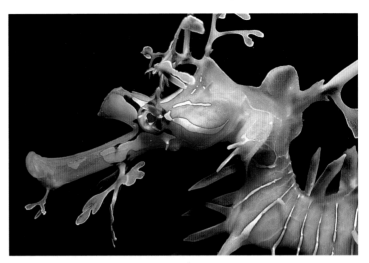

COUSTEAU'S AUSTRALIA JOURNEY

COUSTEAU'S AUSTRALIA JOURNEY

Jean-Michel Cousteau
and Mose Richards

Harry N. Abrams, Inc., Publishers

Editor: Robert Morton
Designer: Ellen Nygaard Ford
Photo Editor: Judy K. Brody
Scientific Consultants: Dr. Richard C.
    Murphy and Dr. François Sarano
Publications Coordinator: Lesley D. High

The Cousteau Society wishes to thank the
Turner Broadcasting System and Amaya
Films, whose support made possible the
expedition chronicled in this book

*Library of Congress Cataloging-in-
Publication Data*

Cousteau, Jean-Michel.
    Cousteau's Australia Journey/Jean-Michel
Cousteau and Mose Richards.
    p. cm.
    Includes index.
    ISBN 0-8109-3187-7
    1. Australia—Description and travel—
1981—   2. Natural history—Australia.
3. Australian aborgines.   4. Cousteau,
Jean-Michel—Journeys—Australia.
I. Richards, Mose.   II Title.
DU105.2.C68   1993
919.404′63—dc20   93-22001

Published in 1993 by Harry N. Abrams,
Incorporated, New York
A Times Mirror Company

Printed and bound in Italy

The Cousteau Society is a nonprofit
membership-supported organization dedicated
to the protection and improvement of the
quality of life for present and future
generations.

The Cousteau Society, Inc.
870 Greenbrier Circle, Suite 402
Chesapeake, VA 23320

*Page 1: A leafy sea dragon in Rapid Bay,
near Adelaide.*

*Pages 2–3: An aerial view in Western
Australia, near Mt. Trafalgar.*

*Pages 4–5: A Cousteau diver with a large
gorgonian that has a yellow crinid on it; at
Clerke Reef, Western Australia.*

*Pages 6–7: A view of Ayers Rock in Uluru
National Park.*

CONTENTS

NIGHT OF THE CORAL BLIZZARD

We had no intention of exploring Australia. We looked upon it as a brief stop for our vessels as they worked westward through serene South Pacific island chains to untamed Papua New Guinea, exotic Indonesia, the fabled Mekong River, and beyond. In our continuing joint circumnavigation of the world by *Calypso* and our windship *Alcyone*—chronicled in a television series called "Cousteau's Rediscovery of the World"—we were intrigued most by places, creatures, and peoples still veiled in mystery. Like millions of others, our image of Australia was skewed by tourism ads, which largely portray it as a paradise for surfers, golfers, koala-lovers, and would be post-American Wild West cowboys. Our only interest, we thought, lay in roaming the vaunted coral realm of the Great Barrier Reef.

We did not plan Australia. Australia happened to us.

Our initial contact with the great southern continent taught us that there were many Australias beyond the civilized land of advertising, zones of land and sea still mostly beyond human contact, still harboring secrets unpenetrated by science and marvels of nature little changed across aeons. We grew eager to probe further, and as we undertook limited missions to remote corners of the country and the ocean encircling it, we continually came upon new and beguiling subjects that demanded investigation. We arrived to conduct a three-month study of the Great Barrier Reef, but the wonders of this strange southern world contrived to keep us for nearly three years, as the vicissitudes of the winds once trapped the earliest seagoing explorers.

When *Calypso*'s survey of the Great Barrier was complete, we decided to explore Australia's western coast, which is oddly overlooked by most of the world's tourist industries and media. However, plans were already in place for an ambitious expedition by both ships throughout Papua New Guinea, so we put aside further work in Australia for a year. When our mission in Papua New Guinea was completed, we returned to Australia in *Alcyone*, while *Calypso* sailed on to Indonesia. Our experiences along the sparsely settled west coast were so compelling that we were drawn to search as well along the southern coast, and that led us eventually to Tasmania, where we came upon fascinating environmental issues bearing upon the future of the whole of Australia. Learning that most of the continent was a primordial ocean parched through time to desert, we conceived of a cross-country expedition by our veteran sailors and divers through the *dry* sea of the notorious Outback, and dispatched a land team in all-terrain vehicles. That journey led us not only into an examination of biological and geological oddities in the desert, but also into an encounter with the mesmerizing world of the

The wonders of the sea are as marvelous as the glories of the heavens.

•

Matthew Fontaine Maury

Encompassing 100,000 square miles, an area nearly as large as Italy, the Great Barrier Reef is not a solid structure but a constellation of more than 2,500 separate coral reefs in a vast array of shapes and sizes. Here, Calypso *sits alongside Yonge Reef, one of the ribbon, or linear, reefs that line the outer perimeter of the Great Barrier Reef at the edge of the continental shelf. Inside the protective wall of corals lies a navigable channel ten to 150 miles wide.*

Aboriginal peoples, who were the first Australians. Aboriginals may have been living on the great southern continent 20,000 years before the first human arrived in the Americas.

We grew interested in the River Murray, Australia's equivalent of the Mississippi, and sent a team to sail it in a houseboat turned exploration craft. We heard tales of the crocodiles and tropical beauty of Kakadu National Park in the far north, and posted a film team there. Planning a single trip, they became so fascinated that they returned to Kakadu five times. While roaming southern waters, we became so intrigued by reports of the area's great white shark population—and by the dearth of scientific information about the species—that we completely revised our plans again in order to carry out the most ambitious and longest expedition ever mounted to study and film great white sharks. (The story of that mission is told in *Cousteau's Great White Shark*, published in 1992.)

Australia enchanted us, and in some ways changed us. By the time we finally departed the continent, one of our two logistics coordinators was an Australian, Ian Chapman. *Alcyone*'s chef, Bruno Gicquel, was a French expatriate living in Western Australia. Australian diver Capkin Van Alphen had become a permanent member of our team, and our engineer, Patrick Allioux, had completed the expedition by wedding a lovely girl from Perth. So much for the concept of a brief tour.

Australia usually surprises those who venture beyond its urban centers and find themselves peering across a plane of red ground that stretches table-flat in every direction to the horizon, softened only by patches of bristly grass, punctuated only sporadically by lumpy rock outcroppings. The erosive action of wind, rain, and heat through time have made Australia the flattest continent on earth. Its highest point, 7,310-foot Mt. Kosciusko in the Snowy Mountains, would be a mere foothill in the Rockies or Alps.

Without scattered elevations to capture moisture-laden clouds and foment storms, Australia is also the driest continent on earth but for Antarctica, where abundant reserves of water are locked up in ice. Australia's largest lake, Eyre, is usually dry. So harsh is the land that less than ten percent of it is arable. Parts of the outback are said to be so dry that it takes forty acres to feed a single sheep.

Australians for good reason sometimes refer to their continent as the "Big Empty." Nearly as large as the contiguous United States, it has only about seven percent of the U.S. population. A recent census found that there are ten times more sheep in Australia than people. Most of the nation's citizenry—80 percent of the 17 million people who live here—avoid its most arid, scorching, and monotonous stretches by congregating in the

(INDONESIA)

TIMOR SEA   *ARAFURA SEA*

Roti
Island

Ashmore   Hibernia
Islands   Reef
                                            Darwin
Scott   Arnhem Land
Reef   *Prince   *Kakadu*
                 Regent   *Nat. Park*
                 River   Kimberley
                             Plateau   *Purnululu*
Rowley   *(Bungle Bungle)*
Shoals   Broome   *Nat. Park*

INDIAN   *Windjana*   *Geikie*
OCEAN   *Gorge*   *Gorge*
                        Nat. Park   *Nat. Park*   N O R T H E R N
                                                       T E R R I T O R Y

                                          A U S T R A L I A

Shark Bay   •Alice Springs
         •Monkey Mia
                                    Uluru
                                    (Ayers Rock/Mt. Olga)
                                    Nat. Park
Houtman   W E S T E R N   •Angata
Abrolhos   A U S T R A L I A   S O U T H
                                                      A U S T R A L I A

                                                          •Coober
                                                           Pedy   *Lake*
                                                                   Eyre

                                                           Lake
                                     GREAT AUSTRALIAN BIGHT   *Torrens*
         •Perth
          Fremantle

SOUTHERN
OCEAN

                                                          •Adelaide

Raine
Island

                                                    Osprey
                                                    Reef

Cape   *CORAL SEA*
York
Peninsula

                    Magnetic
                    Island
                    ◇Townsville   *Eungella*
                                       Nat. Park

         Q U E E N S L A N D

                                       Hervey Bay

                                            •Brisbane

Coongie
Lakes
                                                          PACIFIC
                                                          OCEAN
                        Darling
                        River
             N E W S O U T H
                 W A L E S

             •Mildura
         Murray   Canberra A.C.T.
                    •   •   ☆   •Sydney
                    River Albury

       V I C T O R I A

             •Melbourne

                                       TASMAN SEA

                    Burnie
                    •
                    Gordon R.
                              T A S M A N I A
                    •
                    Hobart

N

hospitable, sometimes lush, coastal crescent along the southeastern corner of the continent. The Australian cities that strike recognition in foreigners—Sydney, Melbourne, Canberra, Adelaide, Brisbane, and Hobart—are all located in this single zone.

Our interest lay in the other Australias, in coastal seas and interior reaches still beyond easy reach of humanity. A series of questions intrigued us and inspired our prolonged stay. What marine creatures endure in seas little altered by coastal development, overfishing, and pollution? Were there living curiosities in the Australian ocean as bizarre as the terrestrial marsupials and monotremes, products of a separate evolution on this island continent? What kinds of creatures survive in such a hostile environment as the continent's interior, and how do they do it? And how could aboriginal peoples have flourished for tens of thousands of years in a domain so harsh that it defeated most of the first European explorers and daunts all but the hardiest Australians even today? Why is it that a country nearly as large as the United States, settled more than two hundred years ago by Europeans, is still so sparsely populated? How has the arrival of Western civilization altered the country's ancient ecosystems? And what are the environmental prospects of a land now celebrated internationally as a leading tourist destination and as a magnet for those around the world who yearn to start anew in one of the last "frontiers"?

We saw in Australia an exhilarating mix—the oldest of the old and the newest of the new. We wondered if enduring elements of the past would soon disappear, as elsewhere, in a flood of new technologies and development, or if the independent and proud Australian people would prove to be determined to preserve their cultural and environmental riches.

In the end, we believed that we understood this land of countless enigmas and mysteries and seeming contradictions, and we found there a measure of hope for all of humanity. In the beginning, however, we were simply curious to see the Great Barrier Reef at close range, descending, as is our tradition, to contemplate and to capture on film the endless magic of the sea.

From the space shuttle, it looks like a vast phalanx of mythological water beasts guarding the northeastern flanks of Australia. From the moon, it appears as a soft squiggle on the earthly face, a recognizable feature as

Coral beds along the Murray Islands, in the Torres Strait off Cape York, represent the northernmost edge of the Great Barrier Reef.

large as Italy and as long as the New York–to–Miami coastline. From *Calypso*, approaching after a long passage from Tahiti, it looked like patches of blue fire in the dusky sea ahead.

The Great Barrier Reef—few realms of land or sea evoke such arresting superlatives as this colossus of the tropical seas—largest living structure in the world, greatest variety of life among any community on earth, greatest diversity of coral species in the sea, largest zone of conservation anywhere, perhaps most awe-inspiring among the great array of ocean provinces, probably most beautiful.

When Captain Albert Falco signaled the release of *Calypso*'s anchor, and the chain descended in a grating rattle, it was the first-ever anchorage of the world's most famous undersea research vessel in the world's most celebrated undersea destination.

Our purpose was not to compete with those who have already compiled exquisite photographic catalogs of this submarine wonderland, but to witness and document an extraordinary annual event along the reef which seems unparalleled in the animal kingdom. It is another indicator of the nearly incomprehensible vastness and vitality of the Great Barrier Reef, and it may be the most engaging superlative of all.

The Great Barrier Reef performs the largest orgy of sexual reproduction on earth. A few nights after full moons of the spring billions of coral polyps across thousands of square miles of the Reef spew a great storm of multicolored eggs and sperm into the currents, a synchronized mass spawning of epic proportions, a great future reef swirling in natal, microscopic parts as a mist of life across a swath of the sea as broad as New Zealand.

Reports of the occurrence give it an almost mystical aura. The spawning begins during a neap tide, which renders the water as still as the perpetually moving coastal sea can be. Then, too, the water temperatures have gradually risen, as if to ignite the fervency of genetic devices that compels flesh to procreate.

Mass coral spawning first intrigued my father, Jacques Cousteau, when he read of the newly discovered phenomenon in scientific accounts by Australian researchers in the mid-1980s. The idea of a *Calypso* mission to document this vital aspect of coral biology seemed a novel and valuable project, and as the South Pacific journey unfolded, Captain Cousteau set in motion the machinery to carry out a Great Barrier expedition.

While *Calypso* was docked for two months of routine repairs in Papeete, Tahiti, Cousteau Society logistics coordinator Karen Brazeau was dispatched to begin advance planning. She chose Townsville as her base and

set about securing the necessary authorizations for the kind of unlimited travel and filming needed by *Calypso*. Brazeau, a Cousteau veteran who has handled expedition logistics from Newfoundland to Noumea, found Australia's customs and health laws the strictest she had ever encountered. She warned *Calypso* by telex not to take on more provisions than needed for the crossing to Australia, since all perishables aboard would be destroyed in the first port of entry. She also sent a note to Simone Cousteau advising her that the family dog, Youki, would have to stay aboard ship as long as *Calypso* was in Australian waters. Such are the varied matters that demand the attention of a logistics coordinator.

From her Townsville hotel room, Brazeau arranged special travel permission for *Calypso* under a convention governing importation of scientific equipment for educational purposes—giving the vessel free access to national waters and eliminating the need for the ship to pass through customs port by port. Then, as the nature of the expedition was defined through telephone conversations with Captain Cousteau and *Calypso*'s project coordinator, Alain Traonouil, Brazeau arranged for the necessary

In advance of a Diving Saucer descent off Osprey Reef, Captain Cousteau discusses the mission with the craft's pilot (and Calypso's captain) Albert Falco, standing in the Saucer hatch. To Cousteau's right is Chief Diver Bertrand Sion, and at his left, near the ladder, Chief Cinematographer Michel Deloire.

equipment, supplies, and fuels to supplement shipboard inventories. All the while, she was working with customs officials to permit the admission of a team of thirty people and their gear, and working as well with airlines to transport team members joining the mission from France and the United States. The worst complication may have been the international time standard. Brazeau was in continuous contact with Cousteau offices in Paris (eight hours behind), New York and Norfolk (fourteen hours behind), Los Angeles (seventeen hours behind) and with *Calypso* in Papeete (twenty hours behind).

Since the ship might not reach Australia in time to document the largest annual coral spawning, Captain Cousteau organized a cinema and photography team to precede the vessel. Cousteau biologist François Sarano and diver Ivan Giacoletto flew to Townsville for advance research, followed by a filming team led by long-time Cousteau director of cinematography Michel Deloire.

During the first week of October, as the austral spring warmed the waters bathing the Great Barrier Reef, the Cousteau advance team set up shop in beachside hotel rooms on Magnetic Island, some six miles offshore from Townsville. It was on Magnetic Island that researchers from James Cook University first discovered the mass spawning in 1981, and the island has been the subject of follow-up studies since.

Small damselfish seek refuge at night among the branches of a soft coral. Like many fish, they bear a different coloration at night. Science has yet to discover a purpose behind this fish's equivalent of donning pajamas. On the darkened reef, the color changes would seem to be undetectable by other sea creatures.

The site was also convenient because of its proximity to the Australian Institute of Marine Science (AIMS) in Townsville, which provided assistance and advice throughout the Cousteau expedition. By charting the phases of the moon, researchers at AIMS can predict a year in advance the period of a few minutes during which spawning will begin. AIMS deputy director Dr. Michel Pichon, who as principal investigator led the scientific team that first discovered mass spawning on Magnetic Island, a man of great cordiality and generosity, joined our mission to share his knowledge of Great Barrier coral biology with Sarano and the cine team.

In preparation for the predicted spawning on October 12, the team secured anchor buoys on the Reef for their Zodiacs. In descending to attach the lines, most of the team caught their first glimpses of the vaunted Great Barrier Reef. Giacolleto, whose participation in Cousteau missions spans more than twenty years, conducted a workmanlike reconnaissance of the bottom while Sylvan Pascaud, a young diver and aspiring filmmaker aboard for his first expedition, drifted about the reef transfixed by its richness.

It is not only corals that proliferate on the Great Barrier Reef. Like rainbow-hued tropical birds flitting about a submerged rainforest, some

Three docile nurse sharks doze in a shallow depression of Saumarez Reef. These nocturnal sharks feed on smaller reef fish and are unlikely to bite divers unless provoked.

2,000 species of fish dwell along the whole of the reef, perhaps the most diverse fish community in the sea. Silver clouds of machete-like sea pike opened in a flash as the dive team passed through and then smoothly folded back together in the wake of the humans, like a marine variant of the Doppler effect. Banded damselfish, bearing black-and-white stripes, patrolled fields of staghorn coral with the look of soccer referees. Barely noticing Pascaud's approach, two sapphire-blue damselfish nearly bumped lips in an apparent dispute over territorial rights. A benign-looking beige cuttlefish, resembling a hand puppet bent in a fist, hovered in mid-water: as Sarano drifted near, the creature gradually redecorated itself in mottled colors of camouflage.

Through all of this Deloire drifted languidly, ever pushing his black-and-silver torpedo of a motion-picture camera before him, ever assimilating for future reference the lay of the underwater terrain, the angles of the sun, the behavior patterns of the local residents.

Biologist Sarano acted as lead diver, surveying the coral heads to identify for Deloire and still photographer Didier Noirot polyp colonies that seemed likely to release their gametes—ova or spermatozoa—soon. Fueled with scientific curiosity, Sarano could barely contain his enthusiasm. After peering closely at a branch of coral, he turned to gesture toward Deloire and in the process brushed his hand against the dorsal spine of a fish lurking under the coral. This turned out to be a dreadful mistake. The creature was a member of the scorpion fish family with an accumulation of common names—firefish, lionfish, devilfish, goblinfish, waspfish—all of which serve notice that the creature can be dangerous. Venom injected from the dorsal fin subjected Sarano to a few moments of excruciating pain, followed by a general paralysis of his hand. An experienced and hard-nosed diver, Sarano neither panicked nor abandoned a dive he had awaited with great anticipation. But his thumb would remain partially numb for nearly a month.

During the day leading up to the night of the corals, as cameras and dive gear were readied, Michel Pichon provided a briefing on the nature of the event for the Cousteau team.

As with many theaters of marine science, what is known about coral spawning seems dwarfed by what remains to be learned. The first and most compelling mystery is why such a massive synchronous sexual act should even occur. In the words of researchers, it seems to defy ecological common sense. When a crowd of individuals from a single animal species spawn together, the opportunities for cross-fertilization are enhanced. But in the case of Great Barrier Reef corals, more than 110 of the 350 coral species on the reef are *known* to spawn within minutes or hours of one another, and

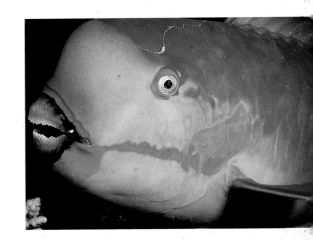

Fused into a hard beak, the teeth of the parrotfish enable it to scrape algae from the surface of reefs.

Opposite:
Along a steep slope flanking Osprey Reef, a Cousteau diver appears framed in brilliantly colored gorgonians, or sea fans. Within a few miles of the reef, the bottom plunges to a depth of nearly 8,000 feet.

research suggests that in all likelihood the majority of corals on the reef participate in the event. What possible advantage could there be in mutual spawning, when an extraordinary confusion of gametes in the currents would seem to lessen the chances of encounters among eggs and sperm of the same species?

No one really knows, Pichon explained. But two theories remain to be explored. It is possible that evolution has devised a strategy of engulfing potential predators in such a sudden flurry of food that they are quickly satiated, unable to consume much of the vast horde of new coral life about them. Ever-ready predators might eat more of the larvae if it were to appear sporadically across days or months.

Another possibility is that the corals can spawn only under a unique combination of environmental conditions, which may occur only once a year. Whether mass spawning is biologically safe or risky, the corals may have evolved without any alternative.

After an early dinner on October 12, the team filled three Zodiacs with the tools of undersea exploration, motored to their anchor buoys, and began a series of dives to ensure that cameras were trained on the coral parents that would shortly begin to deliver a new generation to the sea. Unable to move about and search for mates, corals must rely upon the encompassing currents to act as brokers of sexual commerce. This places profound restrictions on the corals, but it makes the job of catching the act on film easier than documenting, say, the copulation of free-swimming marine mammals. The challenge this night was not to find the event but to be thoroughly ready for it, since for some coral species the entire spawning can be over in about five minutes.

Though a brilliant full moon would cast its eerie glow through the surface layers of the sea, artificial lighting would be necessary to illuminate the tiny coral gametes, and Giacolleto accordingly manned a generator in one of the Zodiacs, feeding cables down to Pascaud, who held the palette of underwater lights and beamed them wherever Deloire trained his camera.

Sarano served as leading actor in the drama, gliding among bushes and plates and mounds of coral to estimate the various times of spawning according to species. Researchers have managed to compile something resembling a flight schedule that lists the predicted egg-and-sperm lift-off periods for those coral varieties that have been studied. Some seem to wait longer after darkness has settled than others. *Acropora tenuis*, a staghorn coral, spawns just after sunset, about 6:00 P.M. Species of *Galaxea* begin issuing their egg-sperm bundles forty-five minutes later. Most of the acroporiid and faviid corals spawn between 8:00 P.M. and midnight.

Since most corals are partially transparent, Sarano could see the egg bundles beneath the tentacle-fringed mouths of some species, an indication that release was only about fifteen minutes away. Sarano, perhaps more than the other members of the Cousteau team, was impressed not only by the scope of the impending spectacle, but by the wholesale changes it represented in scientific understanding of corals, one of the most ancient and prolific animal families in the sea.

It has long been known that corals reproduce in two ways. Through asexual budding parallel to that of the simplest life forms, polyps *replicate*—that is, divide and divide again into mirror-image individuals that form connected colonies in the myriad shapes that comprise a garden-like reef. When a storm breaks off a chunk of living coral the polyps can survive, segment themselves again and again, and expand into a flourishing new colony.

Researchers had also documented sexual reproduction—in which corals generated entirely new offspring that were dispatched into the currents to establish new colonies elsewhere. There is a great long-term advantage in this, since the exchange of genes during sexual reproduction allows a species to evolve relatively quickly to avoid extinction in times of environmental change. If budding were the only means of propagation, a species might be doomed as the conditions of survival were altered.

But it was generally believed that sexual reproduction occurred throughout the year for all corals, despite the fact that it rarely transpired when humans were present. Without realizing the nature of the phenomenon, however, fishermen had often reported pink slicks covering reefs during the late spring. In Japan, in fact, the appearance of red slicks had been known for centuries, and had been invested with a mythological meaning. The slicks were called *punitsu*—"menstrual waters of the princess of the dragon palace in the sea."

When Pichon's research group discovered mass spawning among more than a dozen species on Magnetic Island, a new view of coral birth emerged. Studies found that corals begin developing eggs in midwinter, then in late spring produce sperm. Some corals are hermaphrodites—they produce both eggs and sperm. Some are all female, some all male. As the seawater temperatures rise in late spring, the gonads reach maturity. The importance of temperature is apparent because corals along the inner reef, where the water is warmer, spawn before corals on the cooler outer reef.

When the lunar and tidal cycles are right, the egg and sperm bundles are positioned for release, causing the area around the coral mouths to swell. Probing the reef this night, Sarano could see the gamete balls ready to pop out. Like miniature Christmas tree bulbs, their colors varied by species.

Most were pink, orange, or red; some were purple, blue, or green.

By a few minutes before 6:00 P.M., as light faded from the sky above, Deloire, Noirot, Sarano, and the rest of the underwater team were positioned with their cameras and floodlights aimed at a bed of staghorn coral, *Acropora pulchra*. Sarano had found sufficient distension of the area around the polyp mouths to indicate that spawning was imminent, and he was right.

Almost like clockwork, the polyp mouths began to yawn open just after 6:00 P.M. One by one, they gently pushed tiny buoyant balls of life through their crown of tentacles and into the infinity of the sea. Caught in the beam of cinema lights, the ascending eggs glittered like a swarm of fireflies. Pascaud panned the light across the darkening reef. A starry chaos seemed to be drifting upward in the watery night. When illuminated across the bottom, what had looked like a swarm of fireflies now looked like billions of fireflies. Nearby, the wisps of a sperm cloud rose from a mound-like mushroom coral, the perfect image of a volcanic eruption in miniature.

While focusing on this small section of a single reef, the Cousteau team was ever aware of the magnitude of the simultaneous events taking place at about the same time across hundreds of square miles of the Great Barrier Reef. In astronomical numbers a future coral generation was swirling in the moonlit seas looking, as Cousteau writer Paula DiPerna would later characterize the scene for a television special, like "a blinding snowrise."

Within a few minutes, to the frustration of the camera team, the release of the little balloons of potential life was over. As the men watched in fascination, the blizzard lifted itself toward the surface, where another mystery would unfold. Along the water ceiling, the tail-whipping sperm of each species would begin streaming through the encompassing soup of gametes in search of an egg of similar lineage. Somehow, despite the confusion of species, they would find their own kind. Perhaps they possess a chemical means of identifying the right egg. Perhaps there is some other dynamic at work. The source of the magic is still unknown to science.

When the sperm burrow into and fertilize their kindred eggs, the formation of coral larvae through division and redivision of the eggs can be accomplished in minutes. The result is a free-swimming flake of life that looks much like a tiny jellyfish—the closest coral relative. The larvae drift along the surface for a few days, then descend toward the bottom again, where they are involved in still another mystery. Through some unidentified process, the larvae sense when they are approaching a vacant spot suitable for spending the rest of their lives. They settle upon it, secrete enough limestone to glue themselves in place, develop into mature polyps, bud into a colonial multitude, and, about four to five years later, reach the age decreed by nature when they will spawn en masse to perpetuate their kind.

With repeated muscular contractions, the hermaphroditic giant clam, Tridacna gigas, *releases sperm followed by eggs in jets of fluid that may "erupt" for an hour or more, an act of spawning apparently triggered by optimum water temperature. The giant clam grows rapidly, about four inches a year. When mature, it is more than three feet long, weighs up to 575 pounds and may live for up to 50 years.*

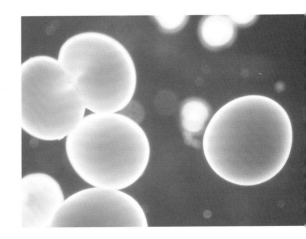

When all of the film was exposed, and the team's energy supplies exhausted, and their imaginations uniformly overwhelmed, the three Zodiacs returned to shore. Someone produced the requisite amount of Australian red wine to toast the wonders of nature and the film that recorded them. Michel Pichon offered a final thought about the mass spawning that seemed to lift the matter from science to allegory.

Most of his fellow researchers believe, Pichon said, that the coral larvae are carried away from the parent reef during the days in which they drift along the surface before settlement. The significance of this aspect of the event is tremendous. It means that most of the new corals on any reef must come from distant reefs. Each reef is dependent on other reefs, and on the transporting medium of the meandering currents, for its supply of new coral generations. The entire Barrier Reef seems a vast linkage of reefs that pass progeny amongst themselves and survive not as local phenomena but as a kind of enormous coral society. The interconnections of all life, one of the principal tenets of my father's philosophy, seem gloriously illustrated in the circumstances of each coral polyp on the Great Barrier Reef—individuals that owe their existence to the delicate and vast mesh of tides and seasons and genes and moon and sea and sun and every vitalizing element of nature, individuals that perform unknowingly as countless components of an interdependent whole.

The Great Barrier Reef, Pichon observed, cannot be regulated as a collection of isolated reefs. It must be managed for the future as a massive interrelated process.

Egg-sperm bundles of the staghorn coral Acropora pulchra *rise to the surface, joining billions of similar baubles of emerging life. Each bundle consists of about eight eggs wrapped with sperm. At the surface the bundles break apart, setting the sperm loose on a quest for an egg of the same species to fertilize. The result is a tiny larva which will drift for a few days before settling to the bottom.*

At Magnetic Island, a staghorn coral, Acropora, *begins to release its egg-sperm bundles into the currents, participating in an annual mass coral spawning undiscovered by science until 1981. More than 100 of the 350 coral species on the Great Barrier Reef are known to spawn within minutes or hours of one another a few nights after full moons of the spring.*

A few days after the events of Magnetic Island, *Calypso* docked in Towns-ville, where paperwork, provisioning, and mechanical tune-ups were per-formed. Since the process would last perhaps three days, Deloire and Brazeau organized a diversion for the film team. Although the Great Barrier Reef was the paramount Cousteau interest, the team was anxious to attempt underwater filming of one of the most curious water creatures on earth, found not on the Reef but inland in mountain streams.

There is probably no better symbol of Australia's separate evolution as an isolated landmass than the platypus, a bizarre freshwater animal found here and nowhere else. Though covered in fur like an otter, the platypus has a rubbery, duck-like bill and webbed feet. It lays eggs like a bird or reptile, yet suckles its young like a mammal. Its legs are equipped with spurs that can inject venom from a sac in its groin. It can detect the weak electrical fields of prey hidden in the muddy bottom using an electrosense system known only in tadpoles and some fishes, including sharks. So confounding to early scientists was its smorgasbord of biological features that when the first platypus specimens reached Europe, researchers concluded that the

A platypus attempts to elude the camera in Eungella National Park's Broken River. Cousteau photographer Didier Noirot spent two days trying to capture the wary animal on film, emerging at last with this single shot.

creature was a hoax. Their first efforts were not to describe its physiology but to find the stitches concealed by some prankster.

To film this living novelty in the wild, the team accompanied two park rangers 250 miles southeast to Broken River, a pool-studded mountain stream near 4,000-foot-high Mt. Dalrymple in Eungella National Park. The extreme shyness of the platypus made it impractical simply to dive into the water in hopes of a chance encounter. The rangers, long experienced in platypus studies, set traps near the entrances to several burrows, while the Cousteau team sectioned off a portion of the stream with nets. When a platypus was caught, they would transfer it to the temporary net dam for underwater filming.

But the subject proved to be as cagey as it is peculiar. The attempt to trap a platypus, expected to take a few hours, lasted for three days, without success. When the rangers decided that the effort was futile, Cousteau photographer Didier Noirot asked if he could try to catch the creature using his own methods. With the permission of the hapless rangers, Noirot drove to the small hotel where the team was lodging, borrowed a 12-foot-long curtain rod, scrounged a hand fishnet from the team's gear, and with the help of the hotel manager devised a kind of butterfly net for platypuses. Noirot, whose powers of observation have been heightened by years of nature photography, had made mental notes during the three-day wait. He saw that the creatures emerged to feed mornings and evenings from their submerged tunnels.

The next morning he wore coffee-brown clothing to blend with streamside tree trunks, positioned himself on a bank near a burrow entrance, waved the rest of the team away, let the net end of his jury-rigged tool settle to the bottom beneath the entrance, and waited for a platypus to emerge. He surmised that he might have only one chance with the wary creatures.

Late in the morning, after Noirot had remained motionless for nearly four hours, a platypus popped out of the tunnel. Noirot raised the net swiftly and bagged it. The creature was quickly carried to the sectioned-off area and released. But someone had failed to secure adequately one of the net fences along the bottom. Before the film team could enter the water, the platypus had slipped beneath the net and vanished.

Noirot refused to give up. He walked half a mile to another quiet pool, located a burrow entrance, and positioned himself again. Two hours later, he had a second platypus in his butterfly net. Now weighted down by heavy stones, the net contained the captive. But Cousteau routine gives first priority to the motion-picture team. In confined circumstances, when a roving extra diver could accidentally interfere with filming, the still photographer must wait until the cine team is finished before entering the water.

One of only two surviving members of the monotremes—the earliest mammals—the platypus lays eggs like its reptilian ancestors yet nurses its young like other mammals. With a ducklike bill, fur, and webbed feet, it is unlike any other animal on earth, and is found only in Australia, where it lives in eastern streams and feeds on aquatic invertebrates.

Accordingly, Deloire entered the stream first and spent nearly fifteen minutes trying to film the darting figure of the platypus through shallow water the color of weak tea. When he was done, the rangers intervened. Acting in their admirable role as protectors of the country's platypuses, the authorities declared that the captive should now be released. When Noirot protested that he had not yet shot even a single photograph of the creature, they relented slightly, permitting the photographer whose ingenuity and patience had made the shooting possible a minute in which to take one photograph of the platypus underwater.

During the last week of October, a Land Team drawn from *Calypso*'s crew set out from Townsville in four four-wheel-drive vehicles—three jeeps and a station wagon—on a grueling drive up the rugged Cape York peninsula. For nearly a week, they would ford rivers and camp amid clouds of tropical insects on an inland mission to document modern and ancient Aboriginal life.

Simultaneously, *Calypso* sailed north into the Torres Strait, which separates Australia from New Guinea. The goals were to investigate reports that natives on the Murray Islands hunt dugongs and turtles, and to search for saltwater crocodiles along the eastern tip of Cape York.

By November 2, the ship had begun to thread its way southward for a general survey of life on the Great Barrier Reef. The first stop drew the team into another spectacle of ocean procreation. Each spring, tens of thousands of female green turtles stop roaming distant corners of the sea and head for barren Raine Island at the northernmost and outermost edges of the Reef. Night after night they surge from the sea like tiny landing craft engaged in a monumental amphibious attack. They ride in on a high tide, then laboriously crawl up the sandy beach and with their cupped hind flippers dig foot-deep holes, into which they deposit a clutch of about 50 to 150 eggs that resemble spongy Ping-Pong balls. As many as 10,000 females have been recorded arriving to nest at Raine Island *on a single night,* and such large numbers of arrivals may persist for several nights in a row. As a result, given the limited size of beaches on the little island, a turtle may have no choice but to dig up the egg chamber of another mother in order to bury her own clutch.

Unable to anchor his ship in the extreme depths around the island, Falco dispatched a land team in Zodiacs to explore the site. Great Barrier Reef Marine Park ranger Leigh Harris accompanied the team, performing a courtesy role as guide but also ensuring that the work caused no disruption of a reproductive event carefully protected by Australia's wildlife managers. Throughout their four-day stay on Raine, the Cousteau team noticed regular

flights over the island by an aerial surveillance team on the lookout for unauthorized visitors.

Lying beside one of the safest entry passages for ships crossing the outer reef, Raine is the site of a forty-foot stone tower built in 1844 to help sea captains negotiate the reef entrance. As the team observed, the tower is today little more than a grandiose bird perch, since for several species of seabirds Raine represents a nesting site as vital as that of the green turtles. Flat and uninhabited, the island is considered the most important seabird breeding ground in Australia. As the team explored the island, they walked below a cloud of thousands of birds. Engineer Jacques Constans counted fourteen species, with gannets, frigates, and sooty terns the most numerous. Harris said that the colony of sooty terns alone numbers 10,000 on Raine. Such a prodigious population of seabirds, Constans realized, was evidence that the encompassing waters were rich in food, perhaps explaining in part the selection of Raine Island as a birthing spot by turtles as well.

During the day, the Cousteau team descended in the nearshore waters to witness the arriving turtles underwater. They found that while birth is the main act of the turtle extravaganza, male green turtles lurk amid the incoming flood of females with conception as a goal. Sometimes, in fact, two males descended together upon a single female.

Dropping backward into the water from a Zodiac to photograph turtle mating and several stingrays sighted by Falco during a reconnaissance dive, Didier Noirot was startled by an unwelcome surprise. When his bubbles cleared, he found himself ten feet from a tiger shark, a species considered the most dangerous of the 250 members of the shark family, along with great whites and bull sharks. The shark made no hostile moves, but seemed to be

pondering the nature of the silver-suited creature freshly arrived from the sky. Noirot's first thought, after the initial adrenalin-pumping recognition of his predicament, was that he did not yet have his camera. By the time he had grabbed it from the Zodiac and returned, the shark was gone. A few minutes later, a second tiger shark appeared and Noirot managed to take one shot before the notorious predator dashed away. Noirot surmised and Harris later confirmed that the sharks were present to feed on weary female turtles making their way back to sea after giving birth. Researchers have noticed that the tiger sharks circle round and round the island in the same direction on their turtle hunts.

The first night on Raine, under the silvery illumination of a nearly full moon, the team helped Harris count nesting turtles. At 10:00 P.M., there

After scooping out a small hole in the sand with her cupped hind flippers, a female green sea turtle lays 50 to 150 soft-shelled eggs, which she carefully covers with sand. Weeks later, the hatchlings will clamber out of the sand and race toward the sea. Only a small percentage survive beach and ocean predators to reach maturity.

were 878 females along a mile-wide stretch of beach. By dawn, the team estimated that some 1,800 females had laid eggs in this small part of the encircling shore.

After returning to *Calypso*, Constans, a marine engineer by training but a naturalist by avocation, sent a telex to the Paris office reporting on the days and nights at Raine Island. "When *Calypso* came to pick us up," Constans wrote, "the beach looked like a landing site, criss-crossed with miniature tracks and bomb craters. Yesterday evening was an absolutely fantastic spectacle, with the hundreds of hemispheric tanks reflecting the moon as they assaulted the beaches, and an unreal battle theater of shadows on the sand and birds in the lunar light."

Some six or seven weeks after *Calypso*'s departure, hatchling turtles would emerge from the sand nests to run a gauntlet of predatory crabs and

Exhausted from the labors of nesting on Raine Island, a female turtle returns to the sea. Once in the open ocean beyond Calypso, *she becomes a living enigma. Scientists know when and where many turtle species give birth on land, but not where they go in the sea during intervening months or years.*

seabirds to the sea. There, if they survived the second set of predators in the water, they would voyage out to live their lives wandering thousands of miles each year through the ocean. Science knows something about the female act of giving birth and the hatching of the young—the two times in their lives when they can be studied on land—but almost nothing about what the turtles do and where they go in between.

For three weeks, *Calypso* meandered southward through the great labyrinth of stone flowers. Hoping to catch sight of another coral spawning off Cape Flattery at Yonge Reef, a site noted for its luxuriant corals, the team spent November 8 and 9—when a mass release was predicted—diving with cameras ready. They found abundant subjects among the throngs of reef fish but no sign of an imminent coral spawning. Under the team's permits for

scientific observation, Sarano and Pichon collected samples of several coral species and billeted them in *Calypso*'s aftdeck aquarium, where they could be continuously observed and filmed in close-up.

As the ship departed Yonge Reef, Sarano filed a telex report to Paris summing up the situation. "Our night dives are in vain," he wrote. "The water is too cold for the coral to release their eggs. Only one colony of *Favia favus*, in our aquarium, appeases us with an explosive spawning that, like a fireworks display, delights everyone on board, but it still can't erase our disappointment."

Calypso pressed on southward along the Ribbon Reefs to Cormorant Pass and a diving spot discovered in 1973 by our good friends Ron and Valerie Taylor, famed not only for their pioneering explorations and documentaries in Australian waters, but around the world. Dubbed Cod Hole for its resident family of about ten large groupers, or potato cod, the place has become a popular destination for tourist dives. Undaunted by humans, the 175-pound groupers mingle easily with divers, conditioned over the years to take food from their hands.

Two veterans of the sea eye one another—legendary Cousteau diver Albert Falco and a giant grouper, or potato cod, at Cod Hole on the Ribbon Reefs north of Cairns.

Once there were twice as many groupers here, but spearfishermen reduced their numbers until the fish gained protection from the Great Barrier Marine Park Authority in 1983. To the groupers, of course, the Cousteau team and its cinema equipment meant just another encounter with glass-faced, bubbling humanity. The stolid monarchs hovered while chief diver Bertrand Sion and Sarano stroked their backs, circled camera-wielding Deloire and Noirot as if following directions on a movie set, and lingered until the last silver fin had left the water, like pugnacious geese anticipating bread crumbs. The experience of consorting with such imposing creatures in the wild was exhilarating for the dive team, but they were left wondering about the residual effect of similar visits by hordes of people. As Sarano put it, the tourists act with the best of intentions, but they are perhaps unaware that they are domesticating the groupers and distorting their normal behavior, perhaps even encouraging the fish to grow dependent on human handouts. At the least, Sarano reasoned, they are upsetting the natural balance of life at Cod Hole. In another telex report to Paris, Sarano briefly abandoned the scientific imperative of calm analysis. "The groupers are dying of indigestion!" he declared.

To survey a reef beyond the reach of most tourists, *Calypso* sailed nearly 150 miles northeastward from Cormorant Pass to Osprey Reef, a lonely atoll that lies seaward from the 2,500 coral islands that comprise the true Great Barrier Reef. Osprey sits near an undersea ledge that drops nearly 8,000 feet within a few miles, and this location, alongside nutrient-laden waters rising from the deep and close to both the open sea and the tranquil reef-studded coast, make it an oasis for countless varieties of undersea life.

In fact, reflecting on their reef survey later, the *Calypso* team pronounced Osprey their favorite stop. Noirot rated it one of the best diving spots he had visited around the world. Even Albert Falco, whose place in diving history is comparable to that of the first astronauts in space, was amazed at the richness and diversity of life, likening it to sites he had explored in the Mediterranean and Red Sea nearly four decades earlier—before overfishing and a host of ecological problems had diminished those areas.

The team glided among extraordinarily large gorgonians—soft-bodied corals—that covered the slopes like a forest of bridal fans engulfed in a sapphire haze. Vast schools of silver trevallies and jacks swept about like mobile, glistening curtains. White-tipped reef sharks patrolled territories along the reef that seemed to coincide with those of huge potato cod, since both of these formidable predators often seemed almost close enough to brush fins. Trafficking among the larger species common to cooler waters were the crowds of smaller, jewel-like fish that emblazon tropical reefs.

Overleaf:
A kaleidoscopic array of corals, fish, and other marine organisms gives credence to claims that the Great Barrier Reef contains the greatest diversity of life in any community on earth. So dense is this assemblage of sea life that it conceals the shipwreck that serves as its foundation—the 365-foot coastal trader Yongala, *which sank off Townsville during a cyclone in 1911.*

Exhilarated by the lush diving, the Cousteau team spent four days here, capping the visit with a series of descents in the Diving Saucer to catalog for the first time the life along the deep slopes flanking Osprey. With Falco piloting and Sarano and Pichon alternating as observers, the Saucer explored three sites to depths as great as 790 feet. They found stair-step walls with numerous ledges and overhangs. Between about 65 and 260 feet, the walls were covered by coralline algae—algae encased in transparent calcareous shells—and soft corals called *Octocorralia* because of their eight-sided structures. Below that, the life grew scarce, dominated mainly by *scleractinian* hard corals, bushy *antipatharian* black corals, and gorgonians. There were trevallies swimming as deep as 250 feet, sweetlips—*Lethrinus chrysostomus*—down to nearly 500 feet, and a few snappers as deep as 680 feet.

In a scientific paper submitted after the expedition, Sarano and Pichon noted that the extreme sparsity of life here, highlighted by the richness of life along the surface, seemed in sharp contrast to studies conducted elsewhere in the Indo-Pacific, suggesting that reefs of the so-called Queensland Plateau off the Great Barrier Reef may conceal a different origin and geological history than those observed elsewhere.

The quest for living space on the reef has left a rooster-comb oyster (Lopha) almost completely covered by an orange encrusting sponge and surrounding corals. Unable to resettle during its lifetime, the oyster nevertheless has all it needs: access to the seawater it constantly filters through its gills to obtain oxygen and food.

At Green Island near Cairns, a park ranger introduces school children to the wonders of the Great Barrier Reef. Recognizing potential threats to the health of the fragile reef ecosystem, the Australian government declared the southernmost section of the great reef a Marine National Park in 1979. By 1983, the park boundaries had been extended to cover 98.5 percent of the entire reef, making it the largest zone of conservation on earth.

From an untouched coral outpost, *Calypso* sailed southward to Cairns, described in tourist guidebooks as the principal "jumping off place for Great Barrier Reef excursions and a world-famous mecca for sportfishing." From Cairns, and to a lesser extent from Townsville and Brisbane to the south, vacationers have a variety of options if their goal is to see the Great Barrier Reef. They can make a quick visit by air, flying out to an island and returning for dinner ashore, or by sea aboard a high-speed catamaran, or they can take a five-day cruise along the reefs.

Near Cairns, at Norman Reef, the *Calypso* team visited perhaps the most unusual of the tourist operations—a floating hotel complete with swimming pool and tennis court, all of which was anchored to the reef by immense

After a short boat trip from Cairns, visitors file onto Green Island for a ranger-guided tour of shallow reefs. The growing popularity of the Great Barrier Reef as a tourist destination poses a challenge for wildlife managers, who must balance protection of the reef with increasing demands for construction of tourist facilities.

chains. They were assured by hotel staff that the structure discharged no wastes to the sea, but National Park rangers were quick to point out that the long-term effects of such large-scale tourist operations, no matter how conscientious their design, were as yet unknown. (Within a few years of *Calypso*'s visit, the hotel had been towed from the Great Barrier Reef, apparently for business rather than ecological reasons, and anchored on the Saigon River in Ho Chi Minh City, Vietnam.)

The general impression of the Cousteau team seemed to support the conclusions voiced by veteran local divers and dive-tour operators—that the reefs seen by tourists along the central two-thirds of the Reef were markedly poorer in life than those beyond the tourist traffic in the far north and along the outer reef. Many sport divers believe that the central reefs have been deteriorating rapidly for about three decades.

It was public alarm, in fact, that led to legislation making the Reef a Marine Park in 1975 and its designation by UNESCO in 1981 as a World Heritage Area. As a result, all but about one percent of the Great Barrier Reef is now protected, although tourism and commercial fishing can continue in many areas. The steps were taken largely to halt proposed oil drilling and limestone mining, which are prohibited on the Reef, but recent studies have also identified coastal discharges and runoff as potential, if not existing, dangers. The problem is that wildlife management authorities suffer from a lack of water-quality data across such a huge and complex undersea realm, and scientists question the meaning of the relatively scant data that has been gathered.

What cannot be disputed is the explosive growth of tourism on the Reef during the past decade, and the resultant increase of construction—marinas, day-trip pontoons, and hotels. Gross abuses and localized effects have been documented, but researchers cannot yet gauge the broad impacts and the long-term alterations that might be underway among coral communities whose biological processes are not yet fully understood.

For the time being, most of the management effort and the dispersal of limited park funds must go into scientific studies, so that a wise and balanced plan can be devised for the future. Few resources are left for day-to-day monitoring of abuses and for enforcement of existing laws, a situation the Cousteau team found worrisome. During *Calypso*'s visit, only 24 rangers were charged with patrolling the entire 133,000-square-mile area of the Great Barrier Reef Marine Park.

There is another peril to corals of the Reef, and it is not caused, at least directly, by human activities. During their brief survey of the Reef, Cousteau divers often encountered the distinctive, porcupine-like starfish

Population explosions of the crown of thorns starfish, Acanthaster planci, *have devastated immense tracts of the Great Barrier Reef. Preying upon the soft polyps, the starfish leaves dead coral heads in its path, such as the white staghorn coral, bottom right. Scientists debate the cause of the starfish "plagues"—some believe they are cyclical natural phenomena; others worry that polluted waters encourage the rapid growth of starfish populations.*

called the crown of thorns, *Acanthaster planci*. Though corals have many enemies, ranging from boring worms and sponges to the polyp-chewing parrot fishes, the crown of thorns may be their most formidable and spectacular predator. Emerging at night, the starfish turn their stomachs inside out, spread them across a coral colony, secrete digestive juices that break down the polyps, then suck up the remains, leaving behind a patch of bald and lifeless coral. One starfish can destroy about fifty square feet of the Reef each year.

But the starfish do not occur singly, and that is the crux of the problem. From 1962 to 1973 and again from 1979 to 1988, crown of thorns "plagues" infested vast areas of the Great Barrier Reef. Some populations numbered hundreds of thousands of starfish, and the damages they caused were startling. On severely affected reefs, the starfish killed as much as ninety-five percent of the living coral.

If the crown-of-thorns has wreaked havoc across the Great Barrier Reef, it has also caused turbulence among the scientists and wildlife managers who debate what, if anything, should be done. Despite years of research, no one really knows what causes the outbreaks. Some theorize that they are natural events that have occurred cyclically across the life-span of the Reef. One research group claims it has found in sediment cores evidence of similar outbreaks during the past 7,000 years. Disputing these findings, other scientists attribute the plagues to changes in the ocean environment caused by terrestrial runoff containing chemicals, silt, salinity, and nutrients. Since the crown of thorns appears to thrive in murky water, there is some thought that increasing runoff may support increasing populations.

The crown of thorns employs a lethal trick to feed on coral polyps. The starfish turns its stomach outward, presses it against the coral, and secretes digestive juices that dissolve the polyps. The starfish appear to be indiscriminate eaters: on some reefs they destroy up to ninety-five percent of the coral species.

None of these potential causes has been proven, nor has any been dismissed.

Beyond the debates over the cause of the outbreaks, there are quasi-philosophical conundrums: since the corals tend to reestablish themselves in ten to twenty years, is there really a problem, beyond the human concern for aesthetics? And even if the phenomenon is universally deplored, what can be done about it short of a massive program to kill large populations of the starfish? Researchers have estimated that a single diver searching for crown-of-thorns individuals—many of which lie hidden in crevices—could collect no more than about forty per hour. Obviously, to make a dent in a population exceeding a hundred thousand would take a herculean assault that seems impossible. The injection of toxic chemicals in the starfish might increase the effectiveness, but would probably initiate reef problems of even greater dimension than the crown of thorns.

In the final analysis, no management decision will likely be taken until the most fundamental question is resolved: what causes the population explosions in the first place? So while the Australian tourist industry and the diving community worry about the future beauty of the Reef, and wildlife authorities deliberate over remedies, scientists resolutely try to solve a mystery whose most salient clues are hidden somewhere between the present day and the seas of 7,000 years ago.

Leaving Cairns on November 20, *Calypso* ranged southward for nearly a month surveying the lower reaches of the Great Barrier Reef. The brilliance of color and the endless expanse of coral had by now become routine, but three encounters deeply impressed the team. While *Calypso* rode storm swells in Hervey Bay, a small team drove inland to film a living fossil that has survived the ages only in the Mary and the Burnett rivers 150 miles north of Brisbane. The lungfish, *Neoceratodus forsteri*, is so called because it has gills, enabling it to live underwater, though it can also breathe air through a modified swim bladder, and is able to endure dry seasons when creeks stop running and oxygen is depleted. Unchanged in more than 100 million years, and descended from lungfishes that flourished worldwide about 200 million years ago, the creature also sports highly developed pectoral and pelvic fins similar to embryotic feet, which it uses to walk along the river bottom. It remains abundant in part because early Australian settlers found it so delicious they introduced it into other streams around Brisbane, and modern Australians have protected it by law.

At Horseshoe Reef and Saumarez Reef northeast of Hervey Bay, along the outer Reef, the team filmed a wisp of a creature that is less interesting

historically but profoundly compelling, if only because the venom it carries is sufficient to kill three people. Sea snakes, of which there are some fifty species, are air-breathing reptiles with flattened tails and other adaptations that make them efficient swimmers. They can remain submerged for up to two hours, enabling them to hunt for small fish and eels along the bottom. They capture prey with fangs and subdue them with a venom as much as ten times more toxic than that of cobras.

Some descents are eagerly anticipated by our diving team, and some are looked upon as disagreeable aspects of an otherwise pleasant job. The dives to film sea snakes fell into the latter category for most of the team, with the exception of Marc Blessington, who harbors an affection for snakes and exhibits none of the aversions to them common among our species. Someone noticed, in fact, that the great Albert Falco changed his routine upon arrival at Horseshoe Reef. Normally, Falco scouts each underwater location extensively in advance of the dive team and supervises the ensuing

work according to what he has personally surveyed below. At Horseshoe, Falco made no reconnaissance dive, and when questioned, admitted with a smile that sea snakes unnerve him. The fact that Albert Falco was afraid of sea snakes became a topic of endless amusement and gentle barbs for days. This was, after all, Falco, the legendary diving pioneer, who for decades had fearlessly glided among sharks, descended to perilous depths, and subjected himself to the first-ever human experiments in living on the sea bottom.

As it turned out, local divers and scientific studies agree that while sea snakes have the equipment to kill humans they rarely do so. One reason may be that their mouths are too small to get a good purchase on the human body. Diving lore suggests that unless they bite a person's ear lobe or the thin flap of skin between the fingers, the snakes cannot get a wide enough bite to pierce wet suits or taut exposed skin.

There are no guarantees, however. The team slipped into the water cautiously—with the exception of Blessington, who boldly approached the first snake he spotted, to the chagrin of his diving partner, Antoine Rosset, whose attitude toward sea snakes is similar to Falco's. The snake mirrored Blessington's inquisitiveness, hovering above the diver's head like a living question mark, while Rosset watched from a reasonable distance. Blessington extended a gloved hand. Nothing happened. He touched the snake's tail. The creature moved a few feet away, but did not depart. Finally, Blessington grabbed the snake behind the head, examined it for a few minutes, then mischievously released it in Rosset's direction.

Still photographer Noirot, meanwhile, followed Bertrand Sion, who also approached a snake. The creature turned abruptly and stared curiously back into Sion's mask from a few inches away. Noirot had chosen to disregard the potential danger of the snakes and had entered the water without a wet suit. As he peered through his camera eyepiece, he noticed that Sion's snake suddenly disappeared. A moment later he felt something odd, and realized that the sea snake had entered the right leg of his swimming trunks. He froze. A moment later, the snake emerged from the left leg of the trunks and disappeared, leaving Noirot unscathed and possessed of an anecdote he would likely repeat with gusto for the rest of his life.

The last adventure of significance came some ten miles off Cape Cleveland near Townsville, where the team explored a strange reef surrounded by miles of vacant, desert-like sandy bottom. Sprouting from a long mound like an alien colony are waving gorgonians, oyster corals, and black coral amid an array of sponges and other encrusting organisms. The fish life drawn to this oasis represent a kind of living exhibit of tropical richness: eagle rays wheeling above a mass of horse mackerel, shoals of yellowtail jacks, elegant squadrons of batfish.

The exuberant but lonely little ecosystem owes its existence to human misadventure. In 1911, a 365-foot coastal trader called the *Yongala* sank to the sea bottom during a cyclone, coming to rest on its starboard side in about a hundred feet of water. The skeleton of the *Yongala* is the building site developed by decades of attaching creatures into a separate and lovely world. For adventurous divers, and for the Cousteau team, the *Yongala* represents one of the most mesmerizing sights along the whole of the Great Barrier Reef.

It also reminded *Calypso*'s divers that the fragile domain of the Great Barrier Reef is adjacent to busy shipping lanes and is subject to summertime monsoons and cyclones. Earlier, helicopter pilot Braunbeck and Noirot had circled above the recent wreck of a Japanese freighter. Plowing into a reef, the vessel had left a scar in its wake for hundreds of yards. Moreover, records show that there have been more than 1,200 shipwrecks on the Great Barrier Reef in this century alone. What danger might lurk in the future for a vast stretch of the Reef, they wondered, if the vessel falling victim to a cyclone, dashed to pieces on coral, were not a freighter but an immense supertanker?

Yet if the *Yongala* evoked worries about human impact on the Reef, it provided ample proof as well of the resilience and vitality of the sea, of the miraculous rapidity with which drifting dots of life can settle and colonize every vacant inch of the sea bottom, and in this clamoring for living space can erect branches and mountains and forests as awesome in their scope as the great pyramids. Wandering into the broken bones of the vessel, the team found itself under the watchful eye of an estuary rock cod at least seven feet in length, a giant who roamed the inner chambers of the *Yongala* like an unquestioned master of the ship. In his territory, under his imperious rule and compared to his commanding presence, this little band of humanity seemed but a meaningless and brief distraction.

The team recognized among the carpet of corals covering the vessel several species previously filmed elsewhere during a mass spawning, suggesting that perhaps as larvae they had been dispersed from a faraway reef—maybe one documented earlier by the Cousteau team—and had arrived here like miniature conquerors of a new frontier. To the team, the lingering lesson was that while we must be concerned about the health of the Great Barrier Reef, in the distant future the relentless, pyramid-building coral polyp legions, simple and astronomical in number, are likely to survive their temporary wounds from humanity, and to return again and again whether or not humans are still around to explore their sprawling and timeless castles.

IN THE OCEAN OF DRAGONS AND MERMAIDS

For most of humanity, the ocean world of this island continent consists of the Great Barrier Reef and a string of picturesque southeastern bathing beaches famed for surfboats and bikinis. But Australia has more miles of seacoast than the contiguous United States, and immense stretches of this shoreline are little populated, little explored, little known.

A year after *Calypso*'s survey of the Great Barrier Reef, we turned our attention to Australia's western coast. *Calypso* had departed on other missions, but her windship sister, *Alcyone*, having completed a study of Papua New Guinea, was ready for a new and lengthy expedition.

We were intrigued by the sparsity of information available about such a vast area. The huge, mostly arid plateau of Western Australia accounts for nearly one third of the entire continent and comprises the nation's largest state. The Indian Ocean coastline that borders it is as long as North America's western seaboard from Seattle to Cabo San Lucas, or Western Europe's shoreline from Copenhagen to Cadiz. About one million six hundred thousand people live here but more than a million of them are concentrated in a single city, Perth. The rest are scattered across an area five times as large as France—an average of about 2.2 square miles per person. It is said that a traveler can cross one hundred miles or more without seeing another human being.

We decided to commit *Alcyone* to a three-month tour, focusing on the largely neglected region along the northwest coast.

On a September morning, Captain Nicholas Dourassoff steered a spruced up *Alcyone* out of the northern port of Darwin and into the tropical warmth of the Timor Sea. During five weeks of drydock primping in Cairns, the windship had been cleaned of hull and keel corrosion and freshly painted a gleaming white. Darwin had served as the new expedition's staging area. Here Dourassoff's sailing crew was joined by chief diver Steve Arrington, divers Antoine Rosset and Marc Blessington, director of cinematography Louis Prezelin, and sound engineer Mike Westgate.

From Darwin, the ship sailed in a southwesterly arc around the mountainous Kimberley Plateau, a pristine wilderness whose remoteness and lushness make it the Alaska of Australia. Diving at scattered islands en route, the team found that the Timor Sea like the Great Barrier Reef was a haven for sea snakes (to the chagrin of Rosset and delight of Blessington).

At Seringapatam Reef they came upon a small Indonesian fishing boat sorely in need of fresh water. Boarding the vessel with a few containers of

A man is rich in proportion to the number of things he can afford to let alone.

■

Henry David Thoreau

A small reef fish rests on a spongy bed along Australia's southern coast. Protected from most predators by the noxious chemicals in its body, the sponge passively filters food from the water that bathes it.

water from *Alcyone*, Prezelin, Arrington, and Rosset learned that the young crew had ventured south into Australian territorial waters in search of sea cucumbers and trochus shells. Though this crew insisted they were doing nothing illegal, they admitted that some Indonesian boats were breaking Australian laws and were perhaps depleting resources owned by another nation. They were fearful of Australian authorities who, they said, often confiscated such vessels and jailed the crews. It was the Cousteau team's first encounter with a phenomenon that has sparked great controversy in Australia and would eventually become a major subject of our films about the region.

On September 27, the team reached Broome, a port city spawned by a pearl rush that began in the 1880s. Broome became the headquarters of the Western Australian pearling industry, drawing together a polyglot citizenry of Malays, Chinese, Japanese, Filipinos, Arabs and Indians, as well as Australians. In the early 1900s, Broome supplied eighty percent of the world's mother-of-pearl. Pearl luggers still anchor in the harbor, though a modern, aquaculture-dominated pearling industry has supplanted the earlier one.

Six other vessels in the harbor caught the team's attention: Indonesian fishing boats. Broome fishermen told Dourassoff that the boats, indeed, had been seized by Australian authorities for illegal fishing, that the crews had been incarcerated for a time and then flown back to Indonesia, and that the vessels would be burned. The team's interest grew considerably, and they determined to document both this curious controversy and pearling as the expedition wore on.

But for now they were eager to pick up American cameraman and still photographer Chuck Davis, who had flown from the U.S. to meet *Alcyone* here, and to glimpse three offshore islands called Rowley Shoals. Local divers extolled them as places of undersea richness little visited by humans. The Cousteau team spent only the day in Broome before sailing 170 miles west to Mermaid Reef, the most northerly of the three.

The atoll, like its mirror-image sisters lying at twenty-mile intervals to the south (Clerke and Imperieuse reefs), rises to the surface of the sea in water about a thousand feet deep. But for a few sand cays which are exposed during the lowest tides, the ten-mile-long oval reef is entirely submerged, a turquoise eyelet in the indigo of the open sea.

A single gap in the reef opens its inner lagoon to the ocean, but *Alcyone* would have to negotiate this sixty-meter entrance carefully on a rising tide, since receding tides gush out of the coral gateway at up to ten miles per hour. Dourassoff sent engineer Paul Martin ahead to scout the passage in a Zodiac

and guide the ship by walkie-talkie. Navigator and diver Thierry Stern climbed atop the forward Turbosail to act as a lookout. Sensing that the scene would appear dramatic from an undersea point of view, Davis and Capkin Van Alphen dove to a position along the coral channel beneath the ship and aimed a film camera at the approaching hull.

What ensued was an extremely close call. Along the bottom, Davis decided with artistic spontaneity to swim to the other side of the channel for a better angle, but Dourassoff at the wheel above had no inkling of the new position and inadvertently headed directly for the two divers. Suddenly, like children before an oncoming locomotive, Davis and Van Alphen had to scatter for their lives, swimming with the fervor of Olympic competitors to avoid by inches *Alcyone*'s double stabilizer fins and whirling propellers. The two emerged from the water unscathed, bearing sheepish grins.

But for this near accident, the diving at Mermaid Reef proved so agreeable that *Alcyone* remained at anchor in the lagoon for nearly a week.

The Cousteau experimental windship Alcyone *passes Raft Point at Doubtful Bay along Australia's northwest coast. The towering cliffs are at the westernmost edge of the Kimberley Plateau, an ancient reef now raised above sea level. The region is one of Australia's least-explored, least-settled areas.*

The crystal-clear, deep offshore waters provided the kind of visibility treasured by undersea camera teams, and the remote reef seemed beyond any influence from civilization, as if still lingering in the mid-Miocene waters that first spawned the atoll's birth. Rich coral knolls dotted the lagoon bottom, and giant *Tridacna* clams and a variety of cones and cowries decorated the reef along the crest of the atoll. Descending along the outer wall, the diving team found a forest of brilliant gorgonians and perhaps 200 different species of corals. Flitting among the coral heads were an array of angelfishes, gobies, wrasses and damselfishes, while moray eels peeked out shyly from crevasses. To Rosset's relief, there appeared to be no sea snakes at all.

Spotting a large potato cod, Blessington and Rosset, who had frolicked with similar groupers at Cod Hole on the Great Barrier Reef, approached tentatively, assuming that the hovering giant would prove wary of divers. To their surprise, the cod turned out to be as friendly as those encountered a year earlier. Later, they would learn that a single tourist dive boat makes occasional stops at Mermaid, and that this particular fish had proven so bold the boat operator had bestowed upon it the nickname "George."

Through the week, George became part of the underwater experience at Mermaid. Inexplicably, the fish took a special interest in Antoine Rosset. Though it often circled the other divers in an apparent quest for food scraps, and once tried to make a meal of Davis's light meter, George seemed to search out Rosset and take pleasure in rubbing against the diver's silver suit. Once the cod attempted to eat Antoine's helmet light, and it often maneuvered into a nose-to-nose position before Rosset, seeming to stare with intense curiosity into his mask. When another potato cod appeared on the third day, catching Rosset's interest, George drove it away quickly, like a jealous suitor. Jokes about this extra-species relationship, at Rosset's expense, accordingly swirled about the dinner table during the week.

There were other delights at Mermaid Reef. During a morning dive, as the camera team filmed soft corals along the bottom, Rosset caught Prez-elin's arm and pointed upward. A lone yellowfin tuna the size of an adult human was slowly passing over the divers. When Arrington turned the cinema lights in the tuna's direction, the beams reflected in a dazzling silver flash. Surprisingly, the tuna continued to course overhead stoically, undisturbed by the lights. When the divers drifted in its direction, the fish moved a few yards away, but showed no desire to flee. The team approached again. The fish moved a few more yards and halted. Prezelin started the camera motor, hoping to capture the rare moment on film. No reaction from the tuna. For some five minutes, as Prezelin filmed, the immense tuna and its silver-suited observers played a slow-motion game of catch-as-catch-can. Finally, just as Prezelin's film magazine was nearly finished, the tuna turned and dashed away.

As the team ascended to a decompression stop following the dive, they stared in awe as a ten-foot swordfish appeared out of the encompassing sea haze and circled them slowly. Prezelin managed to shoot a few feet of film before running out, then tucked the camera against his chest to take a mental photograph, like his companions, of an undersea sight rarely witnessed by divers.

In his personal journal that week, chief diver Arrington wrote passionately about the diving at Mermaid Reef, about beholding the undaunted tuna and the great swordfish along a coral wall far at sea. One passage in particular, inspired by a two-camera dive in which six men participated, captured some of the subtle joys and demands experienced by our diving teams.

"Fish come and fish go," he wrote, "and we rush to cover everything before we exhaust our bottom time. I hear the whirl of camera motors about me. There is no time for daydreaming here. All of us scan continuously for subjects.

"At the same time, we each strive to carry out our individual roles. Louis is doing close-up work, Chuck is filming us filming. Thierry is minding the light cable. Marc and Antoine roam the reef searching. My job is to train the lights wherever the cameras aim, a very demanding task. I must watch the subject and the cameramen, and still be ever alert for changes. I must think about how the light cable is laying, so that it doesn't appear in the shot or, worse, get fouled. I have to stay out of the shots and be certain that none of my bubbles appear between the subject and me. I cannot direct the lights too close to the camera or they will reflect off the particles in the water, an effect called 'scatter.' Since the cameramen cannot talk to me, I must anticipate their desires for direct, side or back lighting. The lights must be held rock steady, so often I must contort my body upside down, sideways or backwards. Meanwhile, I must be careful not to stir up the bottom or drift too near the subject, causing the image to become too bright and 'burn' the film. The hot lights are extremely sensitive, so I must take care that nothing touches them, which would cause them to burst, delaying our work for hours while they were changed. Finally, I must take care not to blind anyone.

"And as my mind is filled with all of these considerations, Thierry gives a gentle tug on my cable. He is pointing upwards and my gaze fastens on the mesmerizing sight of a huge tuna checking US out. The work of being a Cousteau diver is exhausting, but there are sudden moments of immeasurable compensation, when a fascinating creature swims out of all the ocean into my light beams. I love this job."

A scallop at Dangerous Reef sports two rows of brilliant blue "eyes." In fact, the creature's photoreceptors do not create an image, as human eyes do, but are capable of detecting motion, as well as the direction and intensity of light. Such scallops are very sensitive to light changes, and quickly close their shells at the approach of a diver or fish.

Overleaf: Jean-Michel Cousteau befriends a potato cod at Rowley Shoals, three atolls about two hundred miles off the Western Australia coast. Alcyone's team, enchanted by the untouched beauty of the reefs at Rowley, spent a week exploring where relatively few divers have ventured.

There were moments when the burdens of work were lightened by youthful mischief, too. As the routine of morning, afternoon, and night dives became monotonous, sound engineer Westgate surreptitiously hooked up *Alcyone*'s stereo system to an underwater speaker. As the team wandered the black waters beneath the hull during a night dive, they were astonished to hear the sea about them suddenly fill with the blaring sounds of rock and roll. It could have been even more dramatic. Westgate had searched the ship futilely for a cassette recording of the sound track from the movie *Jaws*.

The next morning, Arrington noticed Paul Martin fishing off the stern in single-minded concentration on a beloved pastime that fills the veteran engineer's off-duty hours. Arrington donned mask and snorkel, slipped into the water without Martin's notice, swam under the hull, and gave several vigorous tugs to Martin's fishing line. As the fisherman excitedly fought to pull his prize from deep waters little studied by ichthyologists, Arrington rose to the surface smiling. Martin, alone among the crew, found no humor in the incident.

On the 4th of October, the seas grew heavy, making diving difficult. Western Australia lies in the path of annual cyclones, known elsewhere as hurricanes or typhoons, that sweep down from the Timor Sea on unpredictable paths. Rowley Shoals lies in this cyclone belt, but Scott Reef, lying nearly 300 miles to the northeast, is less frequently affected by such storms, so *Alcyone* weighed anchor, activated the Turbosails, and cruised for a day to outdistance an arriving weather cell.

Scott Reef, a shelf atoll like those of Rowley Shoals, actually consists of two formations, a nearly closed circular reef and a larger, crescent-shaped reef. The team soon realized that they had ventured into waters plied by Indonesian fishing boats. One small vessel was anchored at the reef, another was heading for its protection. Arrington and engineer Patrick Allioux made a courtesy call by Zodiac and were invited aboard the anchored vessel, not vastly different from the sailing prahus used by the crew's ancestors across the centuries.

As early as the 11th century, Malaysian sailors had come south to exploit the marine riches of Western Australia's offshore reefs, initiating a commerce inherited today by Indonesians. As Arrington and Allioux learned, the little wooden sailboats sometimes travel 500 miles from home islands in the Savu and Banda seas, relying for navigation only on the stars and on hand compasses. The crews endure enormous hardships on their six-week voyages. Usually, as many as a dozen men (most in their teens or younger) are crowded onto boats of twenty to thirty feet in length. Unable to carry sufficient food stores, the men live on rice and whatever fish they can catch.

Crossing hundreds of miles of open sea in small wooden sailing vessels, Indonesian fishermen seek undersea riches off the coast of Western Australia. Depletion of local sea resources in Indonesia compels fishermen on the desperate voyages.

Diseases such as cholera take a tremendous toll. But their ever present challenge is to find enough fresh water to survive, a nearly impossible feat among islands mostly devoid of springs or wells.

The crews risk not only death but international legal entanglements. Their goal is to fill each little boat with a half ton of beche-de-mer or Trochus shells, which are valued principally by Oriental button industries, and trepang or sea cucumbers, which are dried and sold as food or aphrodisiac throughout Asia. Since overfishing has apparently exhausted the populations of these sea creatures close to home, the boats are forced to cross southward into Australian territorial waters to find these two living resources in abundant supply.

Australia's wildlife managers permit the exploitation, but impose stringent rules. The Indonesians must employ traditional equipment—no motorized boats or mechanized fishing gear. The fishing must take place within a

Overleaf:

An Aboriginal family from the Bardi tribe searches for trochus shells at an exposed reef along One Arm Point, north of Broome. Tides here can rise or fall as much as thirty-two feet within six hours. The Bardi now find themselves in competition with the Indonesians for the shells—an economic mainstay of the tribe.

strictly defined offshore zone along the outer reefs, and the boats are prohibited from invading Australia's coastal waters.

But Indonesian boats often break the law in two ways. To supplement their meager supplies of food, hungry boat crews sometimes raid bird sanctuaries on some islands, taking not only birds but incubating eggs. And they often disregard the ban on coastal intrusions. In a later visit with officers of the Australian Fisheries Service, the Cousteau team learned that stocks of trochus and sea cucumber within the legal zone are already diminishing. As a result, some Indonesian vessels are venturing into off-limit coastal areas, incurring the wrath of local residents, especially Aboriginal people who rely on trochus shells for an indigenous industry.

Fisheries authorities told the team that the bolder of the Indonesian crews equip their traditional boats with crude motors and paint them black to avoid aerial surveillance, then attempt to poach the still-rich fishing beds of King Sound, a broad inlet less than a day's sail north of Broome. As Neil McLaughlan, director of operations for the Western Australia Fisheries Department, told Dourassoff, the authorities are limited in their enforcement options. "The vessel is the only possession that they have available," he said. "They don't have money, so we can't fine them and send them home in their boat."

Accordingly, faced with increasing infractions and no means to monitor adequately roughly 300 visits a year, Australian authorities impose the only obvious penalty—they confiscate the trespassing boats. First offenders among the crews are deported, and repeat offenders are imprisoned for several months. Masts are removed from the seized boats—which number about twenty a year—and the vessels are removed from the sea to be burned.

A carver on the Indonesian island of Roti fashions wooden goggles, which he will outfit with glass lenses, for the young divers who exploit Western Australia's reefs.

The government permits fishing in Australian territorial waters by Indonesians who do so in traditional ways, using small sailing vessels. Poachers in motorized craft are arrested and deported, however, and their boats are seized. In Broome, Jean-Michel Cousteau examines confiscated boats that will be burned.

Trochus shells polished and carved by the Bardi are sold as tourist gifts, permitting the tribe a measure of independence from government welfare programs.

At Scott Reef, *Alcyone*'s team witnessed not the sad climax of the squalid Indonesian fishing odyssey, but its lively and daring commencement as youthful divers descended en masse to comb the sea floor for curious treasures. The waters seemed like living exhibits of diving history. The Cousteau team in state-of-the-art modern gear glided horizontally among free divers clad only in bathing suits making quick vertical shuttles from boat to bottom and back. The only piece of diving equipment available to each Indonesian youth was a hand-carved wooden goggle with two glass lenses. While the goggle improved a diver's visibility, it also limited his depth range, since water pressure squeezed painfully against his eyes below about twelve feet.

Yet with boundless energy and buoyant spirits, the young crew kicked and pulled their way to the bottom, then darted about the reef to find trochus shells or sea cucumbers. The dappled shells offered no resistance, of course, but the warty sea cucumbers often activated a defense system that must be one of the most bizarre in all of nature. When desperate, a sea cucumber turns itself inside out, spewing its respiratory and reproductive organs and even its intestines at an enemy. The sticky white innards entangle an attacker, enabling the sea cucumber to crawl to safety like a giant, sluggish caterpillar. In about six weeks, the eviscerated organs are regenerated.

While the radical tactic is surely effective with a hapless predatory fish, it proved no more than a source of great amusement to the Indonesian boys, who laughed heartily as they tried to scrape the slimy, adhesive matter from their hands and arms while depositing captured sea cucumbers into waiting canoes above.

Mid-dive, as he roamed the reef filming the chaotic scene, Prezelin noticed a large shadow pass across the sea floor and looked up to see an eight-foot manta ray wheeling overhead. The cameraman rose quickly, gesturing to light-carrier Arrington, and the two divers swam as vigorously as possible to join and film the creature's languid flight. They were within six feet when the elegant manta banked into a slow turn and, with a few beats of its powerful wings, disappeared over the edge of the reef. When they settled back to the bottom, they found Rosset confronting a personal nightmare. Two sea snakes, entangling as if in a courtship dance, were wrapping themselves about Antoine. Soon they peeled away from one another, but not from Rosset. While one snake rose before the diver's face, as if to distract him, the other began investigating his crotch, wound itself around his leg, then wandered up his back. Not until the team had returned to *Alcyone* did Rosset learn how intimately he had been explored by a creature he dreads.

Young boys aboard the Indonesian fishing boats spend their days free diving for trepang, or sea cucumbers, eaten as a delicacy in parts of Asia, and trochus snail shells, which are processed into buttons.

At Ashmore Reef, Antoine Rosset confronts a foreboding scene, a tangle of deadly sea snakes.

Yet for the young Indonesians, the potentially deadly sea snakes were but one more opportunity for recreation. Spotting Rosset's nemeses, they clamored into the water with the zeal of children chasing butterflies through the Bois de Boulogne. One boy of about twelve grabbed a snake by the head and brought him to the surface like a lost pet. To amuse his comrades, the boy twirled the snake around his head like a turban. The creature was passed around gaily and, after ten minutes or so, tossed back cavalierly. When Rosset asked one of the divers about this lackadaisical attitude toward a marine reptile armed with lethal venom, the youth merely shrugged and smiled. Sea snakes were their friends, he replied.

Back aboard the fishing boat, the crew emptied their catch of sea cucumbers onto the deck or tied them to makeshift racks to dry in the sun. Spread across every square inch of the vessel's top surface, the shriveling mass soon emitted a foul stench that further compounded the miserable conditions of the crowded boat. Ironically, the boat crews never eat sea cucumber, which has a fifty percent protein content and could stave their constant hunger. Instead, while living in the midst of a nutritious, if unsavory, food source, they restrict themselves largely to rice and water. Ultimately, the cash obtained from the sale of the trepang will enable them to purchase food that is likely to be less wholesome than the sea cucumbers they gather.

After three days at Scott Reef, the Cousteau team sailed northeast to Ashmore Reef. Though still within Australian territorial waters, the reef actually lies closer to the Indonesian homeland than to Australia, and is therefore a center of trochus and sea cucumber harvesting. Here, the human and environmental costs of the Indonesian fishing were even more graphic and disturbing.

Fisheries Department officer Laurie Sexton, who is charged with policing the foreign fishermen and lives with two other rangers on an anchored sport-fishing vessel, led *Alcyone*'s team to three islets that are protected reserves for nesting colonies of frigate birds, terns, and boobies. Sexton explained that hungry fishermen raid the islands at night, killing some birds for meat, breaking the wings of others so they can be kept alive aboard their boats for future meals. By day, fishermen wander the islets gathering eggs, some of which are carried back eventually to their families at home.

But the fishermen also suffer, said Sexton, guiding the team to an island well clearly marked with warning signs. Dug by Indonesians at some time in the past, the well is now contaminated with cholera, perhaps introduced by a disease-carrying fisherman or a rat carried aboard one of the boats. Though seemingly aware of the inevitable danger of drinking from the well, fishermen still draw water here when thirst leads them to desperation.

During the two-day stay at Ashmore, an Indonesian captain told Prezelin that Hibernia Reef, another forty miles to the northeast, was seldom visited by anyone and was worthy of exploration. The navigational chart on *Alcyone*'s bridge termed it "unexamined," and so Dourassoff took a day-long detour from his planned return to the coast, in part to raise spirits dampened by the gloomy plight of the youthful Indonesian diving crews.

"We have found the most beautiful underwater spot," he telexed Cousteau offices upon anchoring at Hibernia. "The water is perfect and there are hundreds of fishes." The captain's enthusiasm was echoed by the diving team, who had been allotted enough time for a single morning dive but lobbied Dourassoff for a second descent after lunch. The unanimous conclusion at the end of the day was that Hibernia harbored the richest variety of life among the reefs visited so far, including an inquisitive but wary eight-foot shark and a ten-foot-high sea fan pronounced by the team the largest gorgonian they had seen anywhere in the world.

After a brief return to Broome for supplies and fuel, *Alcyone* cruised northward along the coast to St. George Basin, a nearly landlocked bay leading to the Prince Regent River. The river presents an oddly angular appearance on maps, flowing northwesterly some fifty miles in a nearly perfect straight line. The curveless course results from an ancient geological episode. Sometime during the past 600 million years, the pre-Cambrian sandstone bed underlying the Kimberleys—called the King Leopold Sandstone—fractured massively along the present river course, etching a narrow and deep linear groove in the land, which was further deepened over the aeons by waters racing seaward.

Overleaf: Saltwater crocodiles, largest of all living crocodilians, range widely across the northern coast of Australia, and down the western coast as far as Broome. Males have been documented as long as twenty-three feet. Most commonly found in marine wetlands, they also venture more than a hundred miles inland up coastal rivers.

61

The resulting tableau is one of stark beauty, with exposed orange walls of layered sediment festooned in places by waterfalls. Of most interest to *Alcyone*'s team, however, was a note in an expedition briefing book compiled by Cousteau researcher Neal Shapiro, who wrote that the Prince Regent River is home to one of Western Australia's largest populations of crocodiles. A year prior to *Alcyone*'s visit, a young American girl had died from a crocodile attack here. Shapiro suggested the team consider carrying a shark cage with them.

On October 16, with two scout teams in Zodiacs leading the way, the ship entered the river slowly to maneuver among bottom rocks and shifting sandbars. Mangroves lined the banks, backed by boulders that often seemed stacked precariously. The shark cage was not aboard, nor would it be needed. The river was a café-au-lait brown, too muddy for diving.

Four hours upriver, *Alcyone* arrived at King Cascade, a small cove fed by lovely waterfalls. Prezelin was eager to capture the postcard scenery, so Dourassoff ordered the ship anchored for the night near the falls. Warned that the estuarine river tides could rise and fall as much as nine feet, Dourassoff took the precaution of positioning *Alcyone* above a flat mud bank. The film team raced about to document surroundings that were unusually lush for Western Australia, finishing just in time for dinner.

An hour or so later, as dessert was being served, the ship's generator died and the lights went out. Clamboring onto the deck, the team discovered that the tide had actually dropped some fifteen feet. The ship was aground and sinking slowly into the exposed mud bank below.

Under the hull, mud had clogged the water intakes, stopping the generator. The team felt the ship tilt from side to side beneath their feet, and realized that the bottom mud was so diluted as to be nearly fluid. Someone observed that the mud was so soft the team could swim in it. There were no takers, however. As they had filed on deck and aimed flashlights at the surroundings, their beams had caught tiny, jewel-like red spots all along the bank—the telltale reflections of crocodile eyes.

It was here at King Cascade, someone recalled, that the young American girl had died from a crocodile attack. Fortunately, the team decided, there was nothing they could do to remedy their situation by venturing off the deck.

At midnight, a rising tide lifted the ship from the mud, and when Allioux and Martin had succeeded in cleaning the water intakes in the engine room, *Alcyone* moved downriver to the comparatively safer depths of the sea.

A week later, after returning to Broome, we investigated another story involving undersea riches and human suffering. For more than a century,

Less than an hour removed from their natural environment along the seafloor near Broome, dozens of pearl oysters gathered by divers have been measured, cleaned, and set into a holding tank. Recruited from the wild for Broome's cultured pearl industry, the oysters grow in undersea racks that accelerate the natural process of pearl production from as long as twenty years in nature to only two years under human supervision.

this small coastal outpost has existed to support the sea-bottom gathering of pearls and mother-of-pearl—the lustrous shell of pearl oysters that served as a principal raw material for buttons before the development of plastic. Chronicles of Broome's history depict its beginnings in adjectives common to tales of America's Wild West. Rowdy pearlers, like frontier gold miners and cowhands, lived lawless and sometimes riotous lives amid gambling saloons, brothels and dusty bunkhouses. Perhaps more than most greed-driven "rushes," however, Broome's pearling history is saturated with racial exploitation and smoldering cultural tensions among the Asian, European, and Aboriginal peoples who competed for the riches of an oyster species— *Pinctada maxima*, literally "the biggest"—that has dominated world pearl markets since its discovery here in the 1880s.

White European pearlers set the tone by kidnapping and enslaving Aboriginals as the first pearl divers. Skin diving in uncharted waters, the natives often drowned, died of lung infections or untended coral slashes, or were taken by tiger sharks. Ironically, Australia's indigenous people were subjected to injury and death, and were often paid little or no wages, in pursuit of a prize they considered merely a tooth-cracking nuisance that interfered with the pleasure of eating oysters.

In the early 1890s, the copper helmet diving suit arrived in Broome. When Aboriginal divers balked at entering the imprisoning suits, owners of the pearl luggers hired Malays, Koepangers (Malays from the Indonesian island of Timor), and Japanese as divers. The new devices increased harvests, but introduced a new danger, the bends. Ignorant of the biochemical changes caused by increased pressure at depth, owners pushed divers to go ever deeper. Believing the paralysis caused by the bends to be merely a

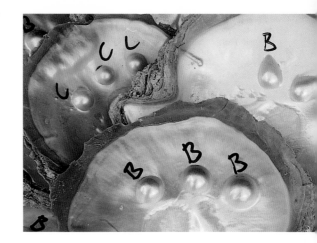

After two years, about fifty-five percent of the implanted oysters have produced marketable pearls, which are marked for size and quality, then surgically removed from the shells.

In nature, pearls are formed when a piece of coral grit or sand gets inside an oyster's shell, prompting the animal to coat the irritant with layers of a secretion called nacre. The jewels are rare: perhaps only one oyster in a thousand produces a pearl. To stimulate an oyster artificially, a technician implants a tiny piece of mantle tissue from a mother-of-pearl oyster and a small bead made from the shell of a mussel found in the Mississippi River. (Australian oysters don't reject the American shell as commonly as they do other substances.)

matter of inexplicable bad luck, divers wore charms and prayed before each dive.

In Broome, Arrington and I spoke with an eighty-year-old veteran of hard-hat days, Indonesian Simon Poellina. He claimed to have dived seventy fathoms (420 feet) in a helmet suit with lead-soled boots. Unfortunately, he told us, the compressor on the lugger above him couldn't deliver air at that depth, so Simon pulled on the air line and was winched up. When he arrived on deck, his eyes were bleeding. To his good fortune, a doctor was aboard and the diver was advised to hang beneath the lugger until the bodily pains he was feeling subsided. Simon remained underwater for twelve hours, and he is alive to tell the tale.

As a Japanese cemetery in Broome attests, hundreds of Simon's fellow divers were not so lucky. More than 900 graves bear the remains of Japanese pearlers, many of whom succumbed to the bends.

As the team and I saw, Broome is still the Port of Pearls, but today aquaculture techniques and modern diving gear have made pearling a relatively safe enterprise. Cruising alongside a modern lugger, we watched from *Alcyone* as divers descended to comb the bottom for wild oysters. The lugger trailed hookah rigs, which continually fed surface air through hoses to the divers, eliminating the need to refill air tanks constantly.

On deck, the gathered shells were sorted and cleaned, then transported to a barge that reminded us of a floating oyster hospital. Here, after a day of stabilization in holding tanks, during which the oysters relax and slightly open their shells, the creatures undergo a delicate surgical operation that implants a small shell bead.

The bead acts as an irritant, generating a process that, until the advent of

The first step in a delicate procedure: after a pearl is safely removed from the shell, trimming achieves the characteristic round shape.

A Broome jeweler displays a sea trove worth tens of thousands of dollars, part of the seventy million dollars a year generated by the area's pearling industry.

pearl culturing, stemmed only from an accident of nature. In the wild, an oyster occasionally suffers the intrusion into its shell of a piece of coral grit or sand, perhaps during a storm or under strong currents. To ease the discomfort, the oyster coats the irritant with layers of a smooth secretion called nacre, eventually building a pearl. The creation of a sizable pearl can take as long as twenty years. Only one oyster in a thousand produces a pearl, and only one pearl in hundreds is of sufficient size, color, and shape to be judged valuable.

Culturing, as performed by Broome's modern luggers, speeds up the process. Arrayed in racks and lowered back into the sea, the oysters are cultivated with the kind of care and experience Bordeaux vintners bestow on casks of a prized red wine. The racks are kept away from swirling sand and mud along the bottom, positioned where currents will stimulate maximum growth. At regular intervals, the panels of oysters are rotated, which helps produce round pearls. After two months, the shells are retrieved and x-rayed. Oysters which show no sign of a pearl are withdrawn for another implanting. During the ensuing eighteen months, the shells are cleaned of encrusting organisms every six weeks by a high-pressure machine. A full two years after implantation, the pearls are harvested in another surgical procedure that not only removes the valued gem but replaces it with another irritant bead to set the process in motion again. Especially productive oysters may be reseeded three times or more.

Before departing Broome, we took time out for an experiment that was inspired in part by Prezelin's desire to illustrate the reality of early hard-hat diving and in part by Arrington's fascination with the old gear. During a long diving career that included naval bomb disposal work and training in diving medicine, our chief diver had gained some experience with helmet suits. In Broome, he found a suit made perhaps at the turn of the century and last used by a Japanese diver in 1973. Arrington brought it aboard *Alcyone*, where he set about rehabilitating it. The fittings were corroded, the rubber gaskets dry and cracked. But with a little ingenuity and some borrowed materials, Arrington had the suit ready for use within a week.

He descended stiffly from *Alcyone*'s swim step into murky water with a visibility of five feet or less, the result of channels sweeping into the coastal waters from Broome's mud flats. Arrington quickly sympathized with generations of pearl divers who searched blindly for oysters through a brown fog. At thirty-five feet, his nearly petrified leather boots hit bottom, and Arrington began a slow-motion hobble across the sea floor while Rosset glided about him clowning impishly in full scuba gear.

Rosset slipped down easily to scoop up an oyster. Arrington, attempting to do the same, found himself fumbling awkwardly in silt, exhausted by the

As Antoine Rosset watches in modern Cousteau diving gear, Steven Arrington labors to cross the seafloor in a traditional helmet suit, reenacting a scene played out countless times during the past century in the murky waters off Broome.

exertion necessary just to bend and reach. Soon another complication arose. We had only seventy feet of air hose, leaving Arrington on a relatively short leash. Above, swells began to shift *Alcyone* about. When the ship swung on her anchor, the air hose grew taut and pulled Arrington across the bottom like a helpless puppet. Just as Prezelin would position himself for a shot, his subject would suddenly disappear into the gloom. To locate Arrington, Prezelin was forced to follow his heel marks in the sand. Inside the old rig, Arrington felt water rising to his chest. So much for helmet diving.

In mid-November, we put into Fremantle for routine maintenance, and the team dispersed to vacations and other assignments. In the first week of February, Dourassoff and a skeleton crew sailed south and east to the island

These "stacks" are remnants of the coastline which has been eroded by the ocean along Australia's southern seaboard between Melbourne and Adelaide. Eventually, as the coast recedes further, these majestic rock outcroppings will succumb to the erosive force of the waves.

of Tasmania, where the entire team reassembled. My father and I, with the financial support of Ted Turner and his staff at Turner Broadcasting, had decided to extend *Alcyone*'s explorations in Australian waters. We were especially interested in filming the bizarre species of sea horses that reside in the far south, after which we would return to Western Australia to investigate intriguing reports about the area's marine mammals.

There are three species of seahorses along the southern continental shelf of Australia which fit the storybook image of these shy fish—with a horselike head, a neck, and a prehensile tail. And there are two species of sea horse relatives that seem drawn from some hallucinogenic dream of what sea horses might be if embellished by a droll imagination. We had seen photos of these creatures—called the weedy sea dragon and the leafy sea dragon— and we were amazed by their exotic forms. They seemed, like the platypus, to be something stitched together out of spare parts. I was reminded of the old description of the desert camel, that it was an animal created by a committee.

The passage across the Great Australian Bight, the country-sized water body along the concave arc of the continent's southern shore, provided a severe test of sailing for *Alcyone* and her crew. Often a kind of wind tunnel for Antarctic cold cells, the Bight attacked *Alcyone* with three storms in five days. Often, waves towered over the windship as it descended into troughs. Below deck, crew members relieved of watch duty clung to their bunks with limbs spread out like spiders on their nets. As crests slammed into the vessel, bathing it in cold saltwater, the frame shuddered and the ship's bell rang out eerily. When seas finally subsided and sunshine flooded the decks, the team emerged to bask lazily as Tasmania hove into view.

About the size of Scotland, the island of Tasmania languishes in the shadow of the great continent above it. Were it not so close to Australia, Tasmania might be better noted and celebrated as an important island. Blessed with more rainfall than the continent, its lush vistas reminded me of England. There are green hills and valleys dotted by quaint farmhouses, clear trout streams, abundant woodlands, rugged coastlines along the western shore, and beach resorts in the east. Less than half a million people live here, and large tracts of the west and interior mountains remain unsettled and only broadly explored.

In Tasmania's seas, cold Antarctic currents mix with warmer currents flowing southward from the Tropic of Capricorn, engendering an odd conglomeration in many places of both cold water species and those common to Australia's coral reefs. Along the south coast, which lies just beyond the extreme limit of Antarctic icebergs, we searched for seadragons among the Maatsuyker island group and in Bruny Island's Adventure Bay, guided by researcher Rudie Kuiter, who holds a permit to gather weedy sea dragons for study.

Making one's way along the sea floor here is something akin to trekking through rugged bush. Blanketing the bottom are great beds of brown laminaria kelp, rootless algal plants whose fronds resemble tough, rubbery ribbons. Colonies of raucous sea lions, little bothered by humanity along these empty shores, rocketed chaotically about and above us as we entered the ocean. But we had played with these undersea gymnasts elsewhere. Kuiter, Arrington, Stern, Don Santee (another American chief diver who joined us in Tasmania), and I sunk to the kelp and probed about gently for the elusive sea dragons.

It did not take long. Within minutes each of us had come upon a weedy sea dragon, and had begun to follow from arm's length its listless journey through the laminaria. Accustomed to fish that dart away in fear, we were surprised by the seeming indifference of the frail, foot-long creatures.

The vision of the little sea dragons meandering lazily above the Medusa-like bundles of kelp struck me not so much as an image of beauty or oddity but whimsy. From a distance, they looked like poster-board cutouts fashioned by a child, then set adrift in the water like wistful toys.

As I approached one of the creatures, and Arrington's cinema lights played across it, my mind conjured up another image, that of a benign amusement-park monster in miniature. Wafer thin, its head speckled bright red and yellow and its neck hatched with iridescent stripes, the sea dragon sailed slowly past my face propelled only by a transparent posterior fin that resembled a tiny hand fan. The diminutive fan vibrated vigorously but seemed inadequate for its task. Little flaglike appendages flew from its head, neck, back, and tail, as if some mischievous designer had added them spontaneously as a frivolous afterthought. It was the most bizarre and amusing sight I had seen in nearly half a century of diving.

I watched Stern raise his hand to catch a sea dragon for Kuiter's research. The fish made no attempt to flee. Stern delicately set it inside a plastic specimen bag held by Kuiter and the two men rose to *Alcyone*, where Dourassoff released the creature into an observation aquarium. Rudie pronounced our temporary pet a female, and briefed us on what is known of these peculiar products of marine evolution.

Sea dragons differ from sea horses chiefly in their possession of leaflike appendages, presumably for camouflage, and in their lack of a coiling tail. In fact, the only flexible parts of a sea dragon are its gills, its fluttering fin, and its eyes, which swivel independently to keep a lookout for predators and the tiny, shrimplike planktonic organisms it sucks up its tubelike mouth when feeding. Like sea horses, they rely on paternal brooding of eggs.

In Adventure Bay, Tasmania, Diver Capkin Van Alphen studies the fantasy-like weedy sea dragon, Phyllopteryx taeniolatus, *whose only flexible parts are its gills and fluttering fins.*

While sea horse fathers hold maturing eggs in a pouch like a marsupial's, sea dragons carry them as a cluster on the skin under the tail.

A final observation, drawn from Kuiter's experience, was that weedy sea dragons do not survive well in captivity. When Prezelin had finished framing close-ups of the motionless visitor, we released her carefully from the swimstep. Like a machine geared to only one deliberate speed, the sea dragon drifted downward like a sinking leaf with no sign of vitality other than the furious beating of its overtaxed little back fin.

A few weeks later, on our return trip west, we filmed the equally outlandish cousin of the weedy sea dragon, the leafy sea dragon, which we found among eelgrass and algae beds south of Adelaide. If the weedy sea dragon brings to mind a goofy, honky-tonk monster, the leafy sea dragon seems its arboreal permutation, as if a strange fish were hiding permanently inside a shrub. From the sea dragon's pinkish trunk hang about a dozen branches with dangling leaves, all fleshy appendages sprouted from the sea dragon's platelike body surface.

There may be no better camouflage in all of nature than that of the leafy sea dragon, Phycodurus eques. A member of the sea horse family, the little fish has evolved a shape that makes it almost indistinguishable from seaweed and kelp fronds, a clever device for avoiding predators in the kelp forests off South Australia and Tasmania.

The extraordinary physical camouflage, which surely makes the creature impossible for predators to distinguish from algal fronds in the dim light of the sea, is reinforced by the sea dragon's rocking-horse swimming motion. Until I was within a yard of the creature, it looked for all the world like a lifeless tuft of kelp being swept about gently by currents. Researchers believe that the leafy sea dragon is relatively common along the shallow, protected seaweed areas of southern Australia, but is thought of as a rare creature because so few fishermen or divers detect it among the kelp. Those residents of the south coast who have seen the leafy sea dragon generally came upon it washed ashore in a clump of seaweed after a storm.

Like its Tasmanian cousin, the leafy sea dragon has no teeth and uses its tube-mouth like a vacuum to suction in planktonic meals. Abandoned by the female after mating, males carry approximately 150 round, pink eggs on the skin under their tails for about a month, incubating and nourishing the brood while serving both a maternal and paternal function. When the young

An Alcyone *diver glides through a three-dimensional forest of kelp along the Tasmanian coast. Remarkably, despite the differences of geography, this same species of kelp abounds also off Chile, New Zealand, and California.*

emerge, they scatter into the encompassing sea looking like perfect, diminutive replicas of the adults.

Found only in Australia, both sea dragons are now protected species. They cannot be removed from the sea for reasons other than scientific research. Once exported for supposed magical powers, the little leafy sea dragon today bewitches only those who descend to its realm with cameras, those who, like us, are spellbound by the evolutionary wizardry of a nature so potent it can turn fish into shrubs.

We arrived along the southwestern Australian coast in time to witness one of the world's most unusual and adventurous commercial fishing enterprises—lobster season at the Houtman Abrolhos off the port of Geraldton. That rock lobsters even exist here is a biological anomaly. Normally, north-flowing cold currents would be expected off the western coast of the continent, which is the case for both Africa and South America. But off Western Australia, the warm Leeuwin Current slips southward between the cold currents and the coast. Though the warm current was identified only recently by scientists, who have not yet determined where it comes from, the Leeuwin was first theorized by an 18th century explorer, who noticed a mixture of tropical and temperate species at the Houtman Abrolhos. Despite the region's proximity to Antarctica, coral reefs dot the southwestern coastline, complete with diverse populations of reef species comparable to parts of the Great Barrier Reef.

There are few commercial fish species here, but there is an abundance of western rock lobsters, which have adapted to the area's unique conditions and use the Leeuwin Current as an agent in their life cycle. Developing lobster larvae are nourished and warmed in the current while being carried nearly a thousand miles southward from the Abrolhos after hatching. Downstream, eddies of the Leeuwin gradually channel the growing larvae back on a return trip to the Abrolhos, where they settle to the bottom and mature.

Were it not for the fearlessness of Abrolhos fishermen, the lobsters would seem to be relatively safe from human pursuit among the craggy and wave-pummeled shallow coral heads that flank the islands like battlefield entanglements. A caylike archipelago of 108 tiny islands, the Abrolhos consist of limestone outcroppings that barely peek through the sea surface (opinions among fishermen about the islands' highest point range between five and twelve feet) and are nearly devoid of soil. Lacking lobsters, the Abrolhos would probably be inhabited only by the seabirds, notably noddy terns, which establish breeding rookeries here.

But from early March until the end of June, about a thousand people

swarm over the barren islands and settle themselves into modern fishing camps. Aware that a rogue cyclone could wash the islands clean of humanity, many intrepid lobster fishermen nevertheless carry their families along for the season, building not only simple homes here but schools and churches. Thirty miles from the Australian coast, they communicate with the mainland only by radio and the occasional mailbag.

It is unlikely that anyone would undergo the hardships if the potential for profit were not great, and it is. Estimates of the money generated annually by the Abrolhos lobster catch range as high as $200 million. The permit fee and gear investment needed to take lobsters comes to nearly a million dollars per boat, but the boat owners who gather the seed money stand to profit accordingly—if their vessels survive the hazards of the venture. Rosset befriended a thirty-three-year veteran of Abrolhos fishing, seventy-year-old Maurie Glazier, who estimated that he would bring in about 33,000 pounds of lobsters during the current season.

Accompanying the fishermen on their daily rounds, we saw that the earnings demand not only a measure of boldness but remarkable boating skills and ocean savvy. Our chart featured a prominent warning for weekend sailors approaching the Abrolhos: "Passage by sight only; local knowledge desirable." What the admonition meant was that venturing blindly near the islands' sharp coral heads might result in the bottom being ripped out of an unsuspecting skipper's boat.

Experienced Abrolhos lobstermen outfit themselves with shallow draft, high-speed jet boats and dash wildly on the backs of waves to drop or pick up their pots before the next crest arrives. Glazier's forty-foot boat has a draft of only eight inches. Arrington asked him the minimum water depth in which he would attempt to work. "Eight inches," he said, "although she does tend to scrape a bit now and then." The maneuvering might seem reasonable in the face of small waves, but the lobster boats of the Abrolhos race to avoid being pulverized by waves that average ten feet and can loom as high as thirty feet.

It is a risky business, and it can be disastrous. Glazier told Rosset of a friend who failed to escape the next wave and barely survived massive injuries as his boat disintegrated around him. One recent season, Glazier said, nine fishermen drowned on the reefs.

A crewman told Rosset of the time Glazier almost lost his boat. A huge wave surprised the skipper, who angled the bow of his boat into the breaker. "The boat went completely vertical," said the crewman, known only as Scoob. "As we punched through the heavy lip of white water, my feet swung out from beneath me as I hung from the steering wheel. Then the bow submarined as we dropped down the back side of the wave, plunging six feet below the water." When Rosset asked the young man why he would subject

Opposite:

Alcyone *visits settlements on the Houtman Abrolhos islands off Australia's southwestern coast. Hundreds of fishing families live for months on the tiny, low-lying islands during the austral autumn to harvest the country's richest lobster fishery.*

Along the submerged flanks of Kangaroo Island, off the coast of South Australia, a vigilant damselfish removes a sea star from its nest. Undaunted by the size of an enemy, damselfish will attack fish, sea urchins, and even divers if the strangers are perceived as threats to the safety of developing eggs. As in the photograph, the job of protecting the damselfish nest falls to the male, which stands guard for two weeks or more until the eggs hatch.

himself to such perils, the answer was simple. "Well, $23,000 for nineteen weeks work is why," he said.

Before departing the Abrolhos, we met Randall Owens, who manages the lobster fishery for the Western Australia Fisheries Department. Owens described the elaborate regulations that are imposed on fishermen—which govern such things as the number of pots allotted to each boat, the size of captured lobsters, and the length of the season. Unlike many of the world's fisheries, this one appears to be managed wisely for a long-term sustainable yield.

Collecting boats roam the islands to gather the catch from the jet boats and ensure its freshness. Bagged a hundred pounds at a time, the catch arrives four hours later at various packing centers along the coast. There workers apply a variety of procedures, catering to the different tastes of their principal markets, the United States and Japan. Americans prefer large frozen lobsters and pre-cooked tails. Japanese consumers favor smaller, steamed lobsters, and prize the uncooked heads, which are shipped as decorative table ornaments. Within two or three days, the lobsters being processed before us might be served at a pricey restaurant on the east side of New York or at a wedding in Tokyo, where perfect red lobsters are a tradition and the smallest shell discoloration can bring dishonor upon the host.

Alcyone departed the Abrolhos on June 4 for Fremantle, where we entered drydock for a minor refitting. Five months had passed in steady travel and diving since our last break, so the crew was rewarded with a two-month leave. Captain Dourassoff took advantage of the respite to outfit the windship with a new sonar and autopilot, and with two new propellers, of a design that succeeded in raising our maximum speed from ten to twelve knots.

On August 21 we left Fremantle again, joined for this final leg of the Western Australia mission by our logistics wizard Ian Chapman and our old friend Michel Deloire, a Cousteau cinematographer who first dove with us twenty-five years ago, left to become one of the premier nature cameramen in the French cinema, and returned for our exploration of the Pacific. We hoped to exploit Deloire's skillful touch when we reached Shark Bay, home to one of the world's shyest marine mammals.

Two days later we rounded Cape Inscription, the northern tip of Dirk Hartog Island, which serves as a fifty-mile natural jetty across Shark Bay and is Australia's westernmost point. Covering nearly 12,000 square miles, the bay appears on maps as the largest indentation in the bulging western coast of the continent. The adjacent land is mostly arid and flat, lined at water's edge by sand cliffs and dunes, and marked by a series of elongated peninsulas and islands covered in saltbush and spinifex. Searching for more verdant terrain and convenient fresh water, early explorers sprinkled names about the bay that immortalized their frustration: Disappointment Loop, Hopeless Reach, and Useless Inlet.

But if the land is harsh, the sea is fertile with life. The bay is distinguished biologically as the site of the world's largest meadow of seagrass—the Wooramel Seagrass Bank. At least nine different species of seagrass flourish here. They are not algae, like kelp, but plants with roots, stems, leaves, and flowers. In total, the grass beds cover more than 1,500 square miles of Shark Bay's bottom.

University of Western Australia botanist Dr. Diana Walker joined us for several dives from *Alcyone*, leading us on a watery tour of seagrass varieties and the myriad life forms that depend upon them. Changing sea levels across the ages flooded flat areas of the Australian coast so often that some

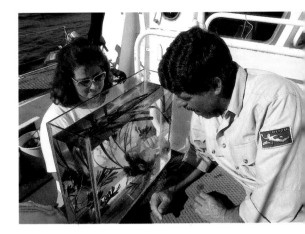

On Alcyone's *aft deck, University of Western Australia botanist Dr. Diana Walker briefs Chief Diver Steven Arrington on the seagrass species of Western Australia's Shark Bay—site of the world's largest seagrass meadow.*

land grasses eventually developed ways of surviving underwater. As Dr. Walker explained, the seagrass bed now acts like a baffle, absorbing water movement so well it can nullify a two-knot current and reduce a two-foot surface chop to calm water. By anchoring in the sand, seagrass stabilizes a bottom that would otherwise shift constantly. The result is a relatively steady, quiet world in which life can settle and thrive. Bacteria, worms, and crabs that feed on dead grasses in turn provide food for fishes, seabirds, and turtles, and the combination of food, shelter, and stillness available in the seagrass meadows makes them an ideal spawning grounds and nursery for fish and prawns.

But the most celebrated resident of the water prairie is a gentle giant that has disappeared from many of its former ranges worldwide—the dugong. The seagrass beds afford dugongs their three most important criteria for survival: food, warm water, and isolation. Nosing into the grass like sea floor vacuum cleaners, they gorge on up to eighty pounds a day, growing to a

Like that of its cousin the manatee, the dugong's passive, vegetarian existence has made it vulnerable to human hunters across the centuries. The largest known herd of dugongs still surviving is found in Shark Bay, where they browse on abundant seagrasses.

length of ten feet and a weight of 800 pounds. As the tide rises, they drift across the seagrass to graze for hours, then depart as the tide ebbs.

Ponderous and slow, the dugong—like its cousin the manatee—has been hunted relentlessly through the ages and fatally wounded in modern times by the propeller blades of careless boaters. Though tourism and recreational boating are a growing trend in Shark Bay, the waters are still vacant enough to offer sanctuary to the largest surviving dugong population on earth. We were fortunate to welcome two dugong specialists aboard *Alcyone*, Dr. Paul Anderson of the University of Calgary, Canada, engaged in a two-year study of dugongs from a live-aboard cruising catamaran, and Dr. Bob Prince of the Western Australia Department of Conservation and Land Management, which forbids dugong hunting in Shark Bay. (The only exception: an allowed hunt by local Aboriginals for whom dugongs are a traditional food.) Paul and Bob estimated that the population was "something on the order of 10,000 animals," a number which surprised me,

A wary dugong shies away from the Cousteau camera along the seagrass prairie of Shark Bay. Despite weighing up to 800 pounds, dugongs are among the most timid of all marine mammals.

considering the scant populations still surviving elsewhere. "Most of the known dugongs left in the world are in Australian waters," said Paul.

Fully aware of the characteristic wariness of dugongs but inspired by the size of the herds, Deloire was eager for the chance to slip among the throng with his camera, imagining countless opportunities to capture dugong behavior, imagining close-ups and micro-close-ups.

But volume, we soon learned, does not ensure proximity. During the entire first week of careful approaches, Deloire and the underwater team captured only a few rolls of the creatures, which appeared on film more like retreating gray-brown blobs in the distant murk than the mammals which allegedly evoked visions of mermaids among early seafarers.

In a telex to Cousteau offices in the United States, Dourassoff described the problem:

> *They are very shy and we have experienced this already. We tried to draw near them very slowly in our rubber dinghies, which we specially outfitted with electrical thrusters rather than outboard motors. Then, we entered the water quietly wearing only snorkels so that scuba bubbles would not alarm them.*
>
> *Till this step all is perfect. After an initial reaction of fear, the dugongs, curious, swim toward us to have a look at these strange fish. But as soon as the cameraman starts his camera, the gentle whirring sound has the same effect as a shotgun. The dugongs swim away as fast as they can.*

After a dozen attempts produced the same discouraging results, Deloire called a photography service in Perth and rented a camera that proved quieter than *Alcyone*'s shipboard model, built in our Monaco workshop more for reliability and durability than what Dourassoff, in broken English, called "silenciousness." The improvement was immediate, and Deloire's spirits brightened as he surfaced with film magazines capturing the creatures from only a few feet away. Nevertheless, as he complained, the situation was entirely out of his hands. The dugong's were directing the shoot; when curiosity moved them to approach him, he could film, when they were indifferent, he might as well return to *Alcyone* and read a novel.

Dugongs and manatees, the only surviving representatives of a mammal order called the *Sirenia* (arising from "sirens" or mermaids) that once numbered twelve genera, are related to elephants, linked by the nature of their teeth, which include short tusks in dugongs, and their protrusive and flexible upper lips, which remind scientists of the musculature of the elephant trunk. But the popular designation for the sirenians has long been "sea cows." The name surely derives from their stout bodies, their herbivorous diets—unique among all the ocean's mammals—and their bovine temperaments. But watching the dugong herd at Shark Bay I found another connection. Day after day, we noticed that many of the animals we encountered were mothers accompanied by a single calf. Like the manatees we had previously studied in Florida and the Amazon, dugong females are exemplary mothers. They give birth to one baby at a time, during intervals of three to five years. Yet they suckle and care for their young as long as two years or more, an unusually long nursing period in nature. Often, we could see calves suckling on their mother's teats, which are located near the flippers, as the adults grazed. The rich mother's milk that swells baby dugongs into plump youngsters and the pastoral undersea scenes seemed perfectly suggestive of herds of fish-shaped cattle browsing across green pastures in a watery western frontier.

During nearly three weeks of exploring Shark Bay, we noticed that many long-time residents bore a grudging resentment toward the rising tide of tourists invading this backwater of the continent. For decades, local resistance blocked the improvement of the only road leading from the coastline highway out to the finger of land that juts into Shark Bay. Only 1,200 permanent residents live in Denham, but in recent years some 100,000 visitors have descended annually on Shark Bay.

The object of the tourists' interest, and of the dismay among many locals, is a phenomenon that stirs in human imagination the exhilarating notion of communication and friendship between our species and dolphins. From Denham, we drove northeast across the Peron peninsula to a tiny settlement called Monkey Mia, whose strange name comes from an English exploration vessel named the *Monkey,* which anchored here for a time, and an Aboriginal word for home, *mia,*—thus Monkey Mia means "home of the *Monkey.*"

By at least 1964, and perhaps earlier, wild bottle-nose dolphins from the sea had begun appearing in the shallows at Monkey Mia where fishermen fed them scraps of baitfish. Apparently, over the years the dolphins gained a trust of the humans along this empty beach and ventured close enough to shore to take food from the hands of fishing families. Some of the individual animals grew familiar enough to acquire nicknames, such as Old Charlie, Old Speckledy Belly, and Holey Fin.

This innocent mingling of people and dolphins has escalated into a numerically impressive spectacle. Not only are a hundred thousand humans drawn each year to the site of the encounters, but about 150 wild dolphins are known to venture in from the open sea at times to play around with humans, then disappear back into the oblivion of the ocean. Occa-

sionally as many as eighteen dolphins at a time gather for handouts at Monkey Mia, gently maneuvering among human legs and permitting their terrestrial acquaintances to touch and stroke them. Since beyond their curious inclination to return to Monkey Mia on a regular basis the creatures do not exhibit any obvious aberrant behavior, and since their robust health suggests they procure abundant food at sea, it is an easy assumption that the dolphins come here simply because they relish human contact. It is impossible to know for certain what transpires in the brain of another life form, especially one whose intelligence issues from sense perceptions gained in a realm far different from ours. But the assumption that dolphins enjoy our company is seductive, and until we know differently, it can only inspire greater interest, especially among young people, in protecting the life of the sea. We were moved, in fact, by the way Monkey Mia's dolphins seemed to seek out children, and to grow even gentler in their presence.

To safeguard the dolphins from insensitive people, rangers supervise the contacts, and a sign prominently displayed on the beach lists the dos and don'ts of interacting with the creatures. Despite the precautions, dolphins occasionally withdraw in alarm or anger as people probe their blowholes or

Under the watchful eye of a National Park Ranger, dolphins and tourists approach one another in the shallows of Monkey Mia in Shark Bay. Publicity surrounding the regular appearance of dolphins here, apparently in search of human contact, draws a hundred thousand people annually to a remote desert shore rarely visited before dolphins began mingling with local fishermen in the mid-1960s.

their eyes. And there is some worry among rangers and scientists that Shark Bay's reclusive locals might one day harm the creatures to drive not only the dolphins away but the tourists who seek them out. A Denham fisherman told us that such a thing would never come to pass, if only because so many of the area's residents fish or descend from fishing families. "As children we were taught that killing a dolphin results in bad luck for the rest of your life," he said. "No one around here would even think of killing a dolphin."

In the innermost recesses of Shark Bay southeast of Monkey Mia, sand and seagrass banks greatly restrict the flow of seawater, creating a shallow lagoon which is about twice as salty as the ocean. In this marine equivalent of an undeveloped vacant lot, called Hamelin Pool, time itself seems to stagnate. Tourists speeding by on the road to Denham, unless alerted to the magic of Hamelin Pool, surely regard it as a watery wasteland. But among the shallows we found ourselves caught up in a kind of natural history "time warp" that transported us back to the very beginnings of life on earth. The complex and exuberant life we had just witnessed at Monkey Mia, in which two highly intelligent and mobile life forms frolicked together, owes its very

Observers have identified about 150 individual bottle-nose dolphins at Monkey Mia. As many as eighteen at a time frolic with humans, then return to the open sea.

existence to the ancient precursors of a unique bacteria clustered into strange shapes in Hamelin Pool.

Wading into the shallows, and submerging our cameras next to the squat, stoollike columns rising from the bottom, we gazed upon the oldest known form of life on earth, called cyanobacteria. Before anything remotely resembling animals had appeared on earth, some three-and-a-half *billion* years ago, in a process perhaps sparked into being by the electrochemical changes arising from lightning storms, replicating cyanobacteria cells formed into small mats and, by trapping bits of sediment on their hairlike surface, gradually built upward layer upon layer into mounds today referred to as stromatolites.

Just under three billion years ago, stromatolites multiplied explosively around the planet, releasing enough oxygen in the process to change an atmosphere that would have been poisonous to most organisms alive today. It was the beginning of the miracle we know as life on earth. Oxygen-hungry animals arose and took command of evolution. But even today, we survive on the same fund of oxygen first created by stromatolites, now constantly recycled by earth's plant life.

Though fossilized stromatolites have been discovered in siltstone rocks inland from the Western Australia coast, and serve as the archival sources of the primordial story of life, the only major population of living stromatolites left in the world are in Hamelin Pool. We treaded softly about them, aware that many of the mud-colored domes may be thousands of years old, having grown to their height of a meter or less at the rate of half a millimeter a year.

The nearly imperceptible growth rate of stromatolites makes them extremely vulnerable to scarring by humans. Since discovered in 1954 during a geological survey, some of the domes have been irreparably damaged by careless tourists. Their slow recovery is graphically illustrated among flat stromatolites at Booldah Well along the western shore of Hamelin Pool. There, wagon tracks traced in the bottom fifty years ago are still visible.

During our visit to Shark Bay, plans were in development to make the whole of Hamelin Pool a government nature reserve. The impetus to protect the seagrass beds and stromatolites here had arisen from concern over the growth of tourism as well as proposals over the years to mine the extensive sand beds beneath the marine grasses. Clearly, such human activities could imperil the continued existence of the pedestal-like structures that represent a living museum of our origins. We sailed away from Shark Bay hopeful that such a priceless heritage would not be sacrificed forever in a short-sighted rush for profits. Humanity, we believed, could afford to let the stromatolites alone in their three-and-a-half billion year epic of survival.

Before leaving Western Australia and its dramatic interplay of enduring natural riches and human exploitation, we decided to undertake a final mission. We had seen and documented the explosive confrontation between Indonesian fishermen and Australian authorities, but we felt that part of the story was missing. We sailed north, crossing Australia's territorial waters, to Roti, the southernmost island in the chain of islands that comprises Indonesia. Most of the crewmen we had met on the trochus and trepang boats had come from Roti, and we wondered what conditions at home had inspired their dangerous, perhaps desperate voyages to Australia's outer islands.

We were greeted by friendly faces and were welcomed warmly into local villages. We watched men hacking and grinding palm wood into the goggles that would permit boys to scrounge about the sea floor for the shells and sea cucumbers that provided meager earnings for villagers. But we saw also the dark dynamics that fuel the pursuit of ocean riches. Heavy population

As part of its Australian mission, The Cousteau Society conducted five expeditions over a two-year period to research great white sharks off South Australia. Tiny Dangerous Reef, a notorious white shark habitat in the sea west of Adelaide, served as the project's most important site. Scientists speculate that great whites are drawn to Dangerous Reef to feed on a local sea lion colony.

pressures have resulted in widespread depletion of local ocean resources, compelling almost all able-bodied male villagers to risk thirst, hunger, cholera, death at sea, and incarceration in order to gather the wealth of foreign reefs and coasts.

For this deadly gamble, an Indonesian crewman may earn the equivalent of about a dollar and a half per kilo of trepang or trochus gathered. Touring a processing plant in urbanized Vjungpandang on the large island of Sulawesi, we learned that merchant middle men sell the trochus for at least $9 per kilo, the trepang for as much as $17 per kilo.

To the boat owners, there is little risk. The vessels are relatively cheap, and the cost of providing a little rice for food is minimal. A boat lost at sea or confiscated and burned for illegal poaching is easily replaced. With a swelling population of impoverished islanders to draw upon, lost or imprisoned crew members are easily replaced as well.

We could see that the confrontation in this remote and financially destitute part of the planet was between overpopulation, want, and greed on the one hand, and conservation of precious natural resources and the delicate web of marine life on the other. For now, protection of the sea seemed to be holding its own. There are still huge groupers and ancient stromatolites, diffident dugongs and boisterous dolphins. But the implications for the future, in a world of rising human populations and inexorable poverty, were chilling. We had visited along the shores of Western Australia a pocket of natural wealth still charged with vitality and beauty.

But for how long?

PEOPLE OF THE DRY SEA

In nearly a half century of diving, I had never descended to the ocean bottom quite in this manner. I sat on a dusty board that dangled like a child's swing from cables leading overhead to a small crane. No need for mask or airtanks. My only special equipment was a plastic hard hat. The crane motor snarled and I was headed downward into a narrow black hole bored into the orange desert floor of South Australia.

I was 250 miles from the nearest seacoast, in a sandy flatland near a rough-and-tumble mining settlement called Coober Pedy. And yet, when the crane deposited me on the floor of a white cavern seventy feet deep in the ground, I was at the bottom of the sea—a shallow sea where primitive fish swam and early invertebrates crawled during the Devonian epoch. I had entered a primeval realm turned by the embalming forces of time and geology into a chalky vault of fossils and stone.

Accompanying a special Cousteau land team that would roam the famed Australian Outback from Adelaide in the south to Darwin in the north, I was being shown graphic evidence that much of the great island continent is a vast and ancient sea, parched through the aeons into inhospitable desert. Across the Outback, scattered monoliths of a hard sandstone called arkose rise from the land like worn red icebergs with most of their bulk hidden below the surface. They are what remains of sediments in the seas of 600 million years ago that accumulated, were compressed, contorted, and tilted by tectonic forces, and were then uncovered and smoothed by the winds and waters of more recent ages.

The monoliths and the creatures interred in the Coober Pedy mine date from a time when present-day Australia was part of the single great earthly land mass known as Pangaea. About 170 million years ago, Pangaea separated into two massive sections. Australia drifted south as part of the supercontinent called Gondwana, along with other connected puzzle pieces of Gondwana known today as South America, Antarctica, India, New Zealand, Africa, and Madagascar.

Like great geological and biological tides, land features shifted across Gondwana and then across Australia, when it broke away on its separate journey across earth's crust some forty-five million years ago. Forests came and went, mountains appeared and eroded away, seas and lakes swept over the land and withdrew. Only about two-and-a-half million years ago, a mere tick in the geological passage of time, Australia settled into its current nature—that of an arid land worn as flat as a copper coin.

The Europeans who came to conquer the vast southern island during the

If you look at it their way, the whole of bloody Australia's a sacred site.

•

Australian mapmaker, on aboriginal religious beliefs, quoted by Bruce Chatwin

As children elsewhere might carry a captured frog, an Aboriginal boy of the Outback totes a desert lizard. The two represent lineages of great success on the dry continent. Aboriginal civilization has survived for perhaps 50,000 years in a harsh world that defeated many early white explorers; and no species has flourished with greater success in the hot, arid interior than reptiles, especially lizards.

past two centuries found that the land rumored since the time of Marco Polo to be a "great and rich" country was a foreboding emptiness for the most part—the flattest and driest continent on earth. Along the southeastern coast, however, they found the country's most hospitable and verdant corner, and eventually established there the urban centers that today contain all but about twenty percent of Australia's population. Beyond the swarm of civilization lining this bottom-right edge of the continent lie lonely, endless roads and scattered, dusty settlements serving the Aboriginals, prospectors, bushrangers, truck drivers, drovers, scientists, and spunky iconoclasts who are drawn to the open spaces and rough life of the dried-up seabed called the Outback.

At Coober Pedy, the lure is a hidden cache of opals, considered to be among the finest in the world. Opal is a quartzlike rock found occasionally among the fossilized remains of the ancient ocean. Formed when silica from decomposing rocks mixed with groundwater to form a kind of silica gel, which collected and hardened in underground cavities and fissures, the

Jean-Michel Cousteau visits with opal miners seventy feet below the desert surface in a mine near Coober Pedy. The opal-bearing strata were formed at the bottom of an ancient sea, and yield not only gems but fossilized marine shells from the Devonian epoch.

gem reflects light waves in iridescent rainbow flashes, as the surface of a soap bubble does. An opal of good quality can bring as much as $800 an ounce, and Coober Pedy sits atop part of the world's largest opal field.

Miners Darren Zechner and Otto Hartwig led me through a maze of deep tunnels, stopping occasionally to point out fossil shells bearing resemblance to those of present-day scallops, snails, and oysters. Zechner operated a machine that chewed through the deposits with whirling metal claws and dropped potentially opal-bearing rocks onto a long conveyor belt. Hartwig scanned for the telltale flare of opalescence at a station where the conveyor belt ran beneath a black light. Peering over his shoulder, I spotted a tubular piece of chalk. Hartwig handed it to me and identified it as the remains of a cuttlefish that lived 150 million years before the appearance of dinosaurs.

The land that now blankets the dead sea of the little cuttlefish and its contemporary marine creatures is not only bone dry but sizzling hot. Temperatures at Coober Pedy can reach 120 degrees Fahrenheit. To escape the heat, many of the opal miners dig underground homes or occupy abandoned mine shafts. There are two motels at Coober Pedy in which tourists can sleep underground.

For human or nonhuman, life in the vast dry sea, as we were soon to witness, demands extraordinary survival strategies, and those who endure do so with earthy ingenuity and tenacity.

Our exploration of the Outback began in the southern port city of Adelaide, where *Alcyone*'s team stopped en route from Tasmania to Western Australia. Dourassoff and his crew helped arrange for two all-terrain vehicles to negotiate the rugged landscape, and gathered supplies for a mission that would often involve camping far from tiny outposts of civilization in the desert. The land team would set out in the austral autumn in order to avoid the harshest extremes of heat, but the trek to Darwin on the north coast would still involve a degree of discomfort and risk. Newspaper stories in Adelaide recounted an incident only weeks earlier, in which a car had run out of gas on a remote Outback road. The five occupants all died of dehydration or sunstroke before they could reach help.

On a Saturday late in April, the members of our special land team arrived at the Adelaide airport from disparate parts of the world. Michel Deloire would serve as the cinematographer initially, to be replaced later by Philippe Morice. Jo Jackson would act as assistant cameraman, American Gary Holland as sound engineer, Australian Ian Chapman as logistics coordinator. Clay Wilcox, an American diver more accustomed to life aboard *Alcyone*, would help direct the mission and serve as a reporter/

Formed in underground cavities as silica from decomposing rocks mixed with groundwater, iridescent opals of good color bring miners as much as $800 an ounce. The Australian Outback contains the world's largest opal fields.

interviewer on camera with Chapman. Anne-Marie Cousteau, based mostly in New York, who had steeped herself in research about the Outback, would act as a field producer and handle expedition still photography, an art she has perfected from the Amazon to Papua New Guinea.

During four days of preparation in Adelaide, *Alcyone*'s crew briefed the land team on their own limited foray into the Outback from the coast of Western Australia. The previous November, crowded into two rented land cruisers, most of the ship's crew had driven east from Broome on a 1,200-mile round trip along a road called the Great Northern Highway. Their purpose was to investigate and to film four unique areas now designated as Australian National Parks—Windjana Gorge, Tunnel Creek, Geikie Gorge and the Bungle Bungle Range. Spectacular canyons at Windjana and Geikie, and a tunnel at Tunnel Creek, cut through a "Great Barrier Reef" of the Devonian era that was now turned into a massive range of limestone. These river-carved slashes in the prehistoric reef are regarded by geologists as classic features of world geology, exposing the various deposits of an

Popularly characterized as "beehive domes" and "tiger striped" rock towers, the rounded sandstone ridges of the Bungle Bungle Range, along the eastern flanks of the Kimberley Plateau, expose the 370-million-year-old sediment layers of a Devonian sea basin.

ancient reef in more detail than anywhere else on the planet. More than mere seashells are revealed in the sheer gorge walls. At Windjana, scientists found fossil remains of extinct turtles and crocodiles—including the bones of a giant crocodile that measured twenty-three feet. While awed by the paleontological significance of Windjana, *Alcyone*'s team spent only a day there, quickly sapped of energy in temperatures that reached 116 degrees in the shade.

At Geikie Gorge, the team launched two skiffs in the Fitzroy River and drifted along one hundred-foot limestone cliffs cleaned white by occasional floodwaters. When the ocean receded from the area, it left behind marine sawfish and stingrays, whose descendants gradually adapted to fresh water and survive there today. River action has dug clefts in the bottoms of the walls, exposing an abundance of fossil shells. With a fingertip, Rosset had traced the spiraling remains of possible ancestors of the chambered nautilus.

In stark contrast to the surrounding countryside, the river banks were verdant with paperbark, mangrove, and river gum trees. The team felt transported for an hour or so to a tropical aviary. White cockatoos flew overhead in raffish flocks of fifty or more, and multicolored parrots squawked from the treetops. Graceful herons and storks walked the shores. Cormorants dove for fish.

As they glided along the river, immense fruit bats emerged from the trees, swirling about overhead like dark spirits of the fish that once swam the barrier reef. Rain began to pelt the team. Looking up, they realized that the droplets were not water but a disagreeable torrent caused by bats voiding themselves. The team members hunched beneath their broad-brimmed Australian bush hats, which proved insufficient as umbrellas.

Along the base of the Bungle Bungle towers, the Cousteau team found marine fossils resembling modern-day sponges and corals. The ancient sponge pictured here, which lived millions of years before the appearance of dinosaurs, seemed eerily similar to those the team had swum among days before off the western Australian coast.

Limestone cliffs at Geikie Gorge are the remains of a "Great Barrier Reef" of the Devonian period, exposed by thousands of years of carving by the Fitzroy River. Details of ancient reefs are revealed at Geikie and at nearby Windjana Gorge in more detail than anywhere else on earth. The fossil remains include species of turtles and crocodiles now extinct.

Members of the parrot family, galahs, or rose-breasted cockatoos, are common along great stretches of the Australian interior, where they roost in noisy flocks.

A day later, in our amphibious bush plane *Papagallo*, I flew over the Kimberly Plateau to join the team at Purnululu (Bungle Bungle) National Park. The setting was as odd as its name, whose origin seems lost to history. Bungle Bungle Range looks from a distance like a mute city of terra-cotta buildings rising from the desert floor. From directly above, I could have been looking down upon an elaborate maze. Perhaps the most striking feature of the rounded rock towers is their horizontal black-and-orange banding, which some have likened to tiger stripes. The dramatic lines are, of course, layers of Devonian sediment accumulated in a vast sea basin and transformed over time into striped sandstone.

Upon landing, I stepped from the plane into 120-degree heat, greeted by *Alcyone*'s team and National Park ranger Jim Wolfenden. We drove to a point along the north side of the range, which is shaped roughly like a twenty-mile-wide stone butterfly. The road ended at a place called Echidna Chasm, where Wolfenden led us on a walking tour. Rising above us more than three hundred feet, the rock walls were broken into a series of sphinxlike shapes and domes by corridors slicing through the massif. Wolfenden knelt down alongside a small outcropping of marine fossils that resembled the structures of sponges and corals mummified and stained by the ages. Once again, we were among the vestiges of an ancient sea.

The Cousteau land team, after bidding farewell to *Alcyone* beside an Adelaide wharf, set out northward on a highway leading 350 miles across the Flinders Ranges to the tiny crossroads settlement of Lyndhurst, then eastward on a road whose name—Strzelecki Track—gave clear indication that it was not a four-lane asphalt turnpike. The map warned against attempting the route in anything less than a four-wheel-drive vehicle. The advisory proved to be an understatement.

It did not take very long for the team to grow weary of the same scourge that had demoralized the first European explorers of the Australian desert. Every endeavor of daily life out-of-doors—filming, interviewing, setting up camp, writing camera reports, cooking, eating, bathing, shaving—was conducted amid clouds of bold, relentless flies. There was no need for an alarm clock, someone observed, since sleep was fitful anyway; flies invaded protective netting, and on occasion a persistent fly would buzz right into a team member's eyes, nose, or mouth at first light, prompting a rude awakening.

The act of again and again brushing away a fly intent on exploring one's face became a constant new aspect of our motor behavior. The passionate swats fueled by irritability during the first few days of the expedition were soon tempered by resignation (and ineffectiveness) into lazy swings of the hand across the brow, rather like the rhythmic motions of a windshield wiper set for five-second intervals. Ian Chapman, who grew up in Melbourne and has traveled widely about the continent, told the team that the incessant swatting has been labeled by native wits as the "Australian salute."

Attacked by flies and baked by the desert sun, the team found itself combating still another challenge—the wettest year in a decade. Alerted to the problems of Outback travel by a heat-induced flat tire on the first day of the trip, the team soon found that off-road excursions (and sometimes middle-of-the-road motoring) could lead abruptly into abnormally rain-soaked patches of the desert. Sudden cloudbursts following ten years of drought had washed out some roads and made travel on others a marathon of slogging. Even our four-wheel-drive vehicles were often stuck in pasty mud

In a dramatic moment captured by Alcyone *diver Steven Arrington in the Kimberleys, a sea eagle dives to catch a fruit bat in midair.*

Overleaf:
An aerial view of the famed Australian Outback testifies to the parched and flat nature of the country's interior. The driest continent on earth but for Antarctica, Australia is also the flattest continent. More than seventy-five percent of the country is little marked by elevation.

for hours at a time. We were forced to take turns pulling one another out in a nightmarish game of leapfrog.

The discouragements might have been more palatable had the initial task at hand, filming the country's exotic wildlife, been more productive. Occasionally, intriguing life forms appeared in the distance—kangaroos, wallabies, and the wild dogs known as dingoes—but in the nearly treeless desert there was little opportunity to approach to camera range without frightening them away.

After 300 miles along Strzelecki Track, the team turned onto a dirt road leading to Cooper Creek. A south-flowing branch of the river, when there is more than a trickle in it, reaches Lake Eyre. This is Australia's largest lake, the continent's lowest point, and, since it is usually waterless, the world's largest saltpan. Lake Eyre fills every five to ten years and retains water for about two years. During its sporadic floodings, an entire ecosystem comes to life, with resident creatures emerging from dried mud and migrant birds flying in from great distances.

The other branch of Cooper Creek empties to the northwest into Coongie Lake and a series of connected lakes beyond it known as the Coongie Lakes. To Jake Gillen, an agronomist who has studied Coongie Lakes, they are "a

A dingo settles into desert grasses to keep a watch for movement indicating a potential meal. Wild dogs that roam the interior, dingoes are believed to have been brought to Australia as domestic pets by early seafaring immigrants from Asia.

string of watery pearls draped across the desert." But the pearls are only partly watery and only on an unpredictable schedule. While some of the lakes may contain water at any one time, the only permanent repositories are a few water holes that dot the region. These holes act as refuges for the eleven species of fish that dwell in the lakes. The fish withdraw to the water holes during extended droughts and their populations contract. As the lakes fill, the fish populations expand with the waters.

At Cooper Creek, the team met up with field biologist Dr. Julian Reid, who is studying the natural history of Coongie Lakes along with Gillen to devise a strategy for protecting them from an influx of tourists in four-wheel-drive vehicles, as well as from oil exploration crews. Reid took the team on a long Zodiac cruise, introducing his visitors to animals that have solved the problems of surviving in what the scientist gauges to be one of the most unpredictable ecosystems in the world. The average annual rainfall here seldom exceeds five inches, and that can plop onto the landscape in a single storm. Years of drought can pass, then be broken by a single year of abundant water.

Frogs thrive in this changing milieu of mud, cracked dirt, and flood. The Coongie Lakes, in fact, support central Australia's richest frog community. Reid caught a small, speckled frog at the edge of the lake and held it up admiringly. Called the trilling frog, the creature buries itself as deep as three feet in mud when the lake is subsiding, cloaks itself in its loose skin, undergoes a deceleration in its metabolism rate, and waits as long as several years for the next flood. The Aboriginals who once lived along Coongie Lakes shores used the frogs as emergency canteens. When no other source of water could be found to quench thirst, they dug up a frog and squeezed the water from it.

The variety and number of birds (more than 150 species and at least 20,000 individuals) drawn to Coongie Lakes are extraordinary in the midst of such an arid zone. Little white corellas, known elsewhere as parakeets, perched like blossoms in gum and coolibah trees. Hundreds of galahs, pink and gray cockatoos found commonly throughout Australia, swept overhead in flocks. Yellow-billed spoonbills scouted from bankside trees for fish dinners.

Reid told the team that rising waters would soon attract thousands of ducks, including an endangered species called the freckled duck, and perhaps three or four thousand black swans. While Anne-Marie and Deloire aimed their cameras, Reid eased the Zodiac toward a floating assemblage of fish eaters more commonly associated with seacoasts. In their characteristic ungainly takeoff, white-and-black pelicans rose from the lake surface to flap silently away from the approaching humans and

To survive the searing heat of the Australian interior deserts, many amphibians like this frog burrow underground, where bodily water is preserved, and emerge only after rains to feed and mate.

Overleaf:
Photographed from the air by expedition still photographer Anne-Marie Cousteau are a portion of the 60,000 banded stilts seen nesting on an island in Lake Torrens during the Cousteau team's trek through central Australia. Little is known about the breeding of these nomadic birds.

settle indignantly in the distance. Reid told the team that thousands of Australian pelicans are part of the Coongie Lakes community, opportunistically moving from lake to lake, or to water hole, as the fish shift about with the waters.

Watching the pterosaurlike glide of the pelicans across Coongie Lake, Deloire was reminded that flying dinosaurs hunted fish over the shallow primeval seas that once covered inland Australia. A camera transported backward in time a hundred million years, he observed, might capture a similar scene at the same place.

After two weeks exploring Coongie Lakes, the team made its way southwest to document an event that was generating excitement among Australian bird researchers. The subject was a bird called the banded stilt, a wader with long slender legs and an awllike beak used to probe or sweep about for its favorite food, brine shrimps. The bird intrigues scientists because it is highly nomadic, and its movements, beyond a general tendency to move coastward in summer, seem erratic. Accordingly, since the whereabouts of its colonies vary mysteriously, banded stilt breeding has seldom been observed. It is known to occur irregularly in lakes of southern Australia, probably wherever conditions of good water level and food prevail.

The year of our arrival turned out to be a lucky one for science. The uncharacteristically heavy rains that trapped our land cruisers in mud had also swollen otherwise anemic rivers to such an extent that water was flooding where water seldom went. Lake Torrens, nearly as large as Lake Eyre, was filling with water for the first time in one hundred years. And settled on an island in Lake Torrens was a raucous colony of 60,000 banded stilts—breeding.

Since few roads reach the shore of Lake Torrens and some of those were impassable, the team chartered a plane so that Deloire and Anne-Marie could capture the rare sight in aerial film and stills. From above, they could see not only the chaos of white-and-black stilts commuting between food and nests, but flocks of gulls waiting for opportunities to dash into the colony and make off with eggs and chicks.

For Anne-Marie and Deloire, the view from high in the air was as remarkable as the life-and-death struggles going on below. The century-dry lake was now a sheet of water stretching toward the horizon as smooth and silver as a great mirror, still another reminder of the ancient sea. Outsiders from half a world away, the two felt blessed by serendipitous good fortune to behold and document a phenomenon that occurs so rarely. How many people had lived and died across decades in the sparse settlements below without ever witnessing the beauty of Torrens in its rare manifestation as a lake with water in it?

From Torrens, the Cousteau team drove westward to Stuart Highway, which was paved mostly by the U.S. Army during World War II and is the main artery leading north/south through the entire midsection of the continent. Australians call the two-lane road simply "The Track." The flatness of the terrain it crosses was soon evident in the truck trains encountered by the team along the highway. With no steep grades or sharp curves to negotiate, truckers string together caravan-like files of trailers behind their tractors. A forty-four-wheel, ten-trailer truck barreling through the vacant desert was not an uncommon sight.

Heading north toward Alice Springs, long celebrated as the boisterous town in the empty red heart of the continent, the team entered a world of extremes where seasonal temperatures can dip to the freezing point at night and reach 120 degrees Fahrenheit at midday. It is not a realm for orchids and flamingos. To survive here, life must find ways to endure or to escape some of nature's harshest trials.

Venturing off the main road, the team soon realized that two kinds of creatures in particular have solved the problems of staying alive in the Outback—insects and reptiles. Numbers offer the first proof. There are 54,000 species of insects in Australia and more native species of lizards than birds. Some retreat underground to avoid being broiled or desiccated,

Termite mounds rise from the desert floor at the eastern edge of the Kimberley district. Among the most accomplished architects in nature, termites create their own self-contained environment within the towering mud nests, enabling them to escape the desiccating heat of the Outback.

Green tree ants, like termites, build their own insulated habitat to avoid the harsh extremes of the desert. Aboriginals, who learned to exploit the environment for all of their needs, use these nests as nasal decongestants. They squeeze the leaf structure in their hands and inhale aromatic compounds concentrated in the bodies of the ants.

including many of the continent's 4,000 species of ants. There are more ant species in Australia's deserts than in any other arid region of the world.

Perhaps the most creative and durable of the insect hordes, however, are termites, which we would encounter with increasing frequency in the more tropical northern stretches of the outback. Together with cockroaches, termites preceded the appearance of social insects like ants and bees by tens of millions of years, and probably organized the world's first insect colonies. Most of Australia's 350 termite species build underground nests, but others erect architectural wonders, skyscraper mounds that rise as high as twenty feet, feature intricate tunnel highways and residential galleries, and house up to a million or more individuals. The mud-colored castles, fashioned from soil and saliva, enable the termites to seal out the desert and create a self-contained climate, like miniature astronauts on an alien planet. Not only do the mud cases provide shelter from heat, cold, blazing sunlight, and cloudbursts, but they maintain an inner humidity of ninety percent despite the parched world that surrounds them.

The proliferation of ants and termites makes life possible for another highly specialized and bizarre creature, the echidna. Found only in Australia and New Guinea, the echidna is most closely related to the platypus, the only other surviving member of the monotremes, egg-laying, toothless mammals. Retaining many of the features of reptilian ancestors, they perhaps represent evolutionary throwbacks to the earliest of all mammals. Resembling a living ball of protective spines, the echidna shelters in crevices during the heat of day, then uses its powerful front claws to tear

Despite its formidable name, the thorny devil poses a threat only to the ants on which it feeds. Spines on its body serve a dual purpose in the desert: deterring potential predators, and channeling nighttime dew along skin furrows to the creature's mouth, an extraordinary invention of evolution that helps the reptile survive in an arid land.

open the nests of ants and termites, which it collects on a long, sticky tongue.

It is hard to top the adaptive superiority of Australia's reptiles, however. The continent has even been called "the land of reptiles." An array of lizards roam the Outback like skittish overlords, cloaked in exotic camouflage and adornments, ranging in size from two-inch skinks to eight-foot monitors, which look like small dragons and were thought of by early explorers as terrestrial crocodiles.

As cold-blooded creatures, reptiles absorb and thrive on heat that threatens mammals, acting to moderate excess heat by moving to the shade or going underground. But evolution has prepared them for desert harshness with other bodily accessories. The skin of many reptiles changes color according to the time of day, turning light to reflect the midday sun and dark to absorb heat in the morning and evening, as humans change from a T-shirt to a sweater. Generally, their undersides are pale to help deflect heat radiating from the ground. Behavior helps, too. The speed with which lizards run, for example, and their tiptoe steps, minimize contact with the hot desert floor.

One curious little lizard, called the thorny devil because of its ferocious-looking spikes and horns, takes adaptation to a high level of refinement. In waterless terrain, the devil's body collects tiny drops of nighttime dew and conveys the moisture along a capillary network to the creature's mouth.

Perhaps the most celebrated residents of central Australia are not its omnipresent lizards but members of the kangaroo family, symbols of the

The frilled lizard of the Outback, measuring about two feet from snout to tip of tail, projects a ferocious image that is all bluff. Folds of skin around its neck can be erected to frighten away enemies.

entire continent to schoolchildren around the world and sources of excitement to foreign occupants of the tour buses that increasingly speed toward Alice Springs on Stuart Highway. With evolutionary tenacity, they have clung to Australia as the continent shifted through the aeons from a lushly forested land to its present aridity, changing in the process from mouse-sized insect-eaters to the large plains kangaroos and agile rock wallabies of today. However, it was not their marsupial pouches and storybook appearances that interested our team so much as their ability to cope with a hostile environment seemingly better suited to insects and reptiles.

Pulling to the side of the road, the Cousteau team often studied the shy creatures from afar. Alertly raising their heads and ears, like the deer and antelopes whose niche they fill in Australia, red kangaroos stared back for a time, then resumed grazing the sparse desert grasses. Similarly, where stony outcrops rose, yellow-footed rock wallabies kept a lookout on the visitors while perched in the security of their steep, high ground. But for a few anatomical differences relating to their preferred habitats, and the superior size of most kangaroos, there is little difference between these close cousins. In the hottest part of the day, the team noticed, the creatures spent a great deal of time licking their forearms. The strange behavior, we were to learn later, is a kangaroo and wallaby equivalent of air conditioning. Their forearms are rich in tiny capillaries. As saliva from their tongues evaporates, it helps draw heat from the capillaries, which serve as a kind of organic radiator.

Kangaroos employ other cooling tricks, as well, such as keeping their long tails tucked into the shade beneath their bodies and constantly panting

Equipped by evolution with powerful hind legs that act as springs, the kangaroo is well suited to the Australian bush. Able to travel long distances using relatively little energy, kangaroos can escape predators in a land with few hiding places, and can move quickly to new grazing sites as sporadic storms irrigate patches of desert grass.

through their noses, as dogs regulate heat by panting through their mouths. Even their powerful hind legs, which serve predominantly as tools of escape, contribute to their durability in this seared land. Not only can they cover a great deal of territory relatively quickly, enabling them to move nomadically to patches of grass newly irrigated by widely scattered rains, but the spring-like mechanisms of their hind legs accomplish this travel with relatively low expenditures of energy, making kangaroos highly efficient exploiters of the Outback's limited food supplies.

Eleven-hundred miles north of Adelaide, Stuart Highway passes through an area known to Australians as the Red Center, where ferrous earth lies in striking contrast to the overarching deep blue of the desert sky. At Alice Springs—called affectionately "The Alice" by Outback dwellers—the Cousteau team took a respite from overnight camping, spending two weeks in a motel and using the little desert capital as a base for exploring.

Founded in 1872 as a repeater station along the Adelaide-to-Darwin overland telegraph, The Alice is celebrated in Outback lore as an outpost of beer-drinking, desert-loving, rugged individualists, but the team found it undergoing a bush version of gentrification. Inspired by tourism and population growth, the town boasted a recently installed set of traffic lights and a new concrete mall. Still, for all its attempts to modernize, Alice Springs remains a lonely island of neon and small museums in a sea of empty terrain that begins at the edge of town.

Two of the tourist attractions here reveal the difficulty with which the first European arrivals adjusted to the Outback environment, in contrast to the elaborately adapted desert flora and fauna around them. Fueled by confidence in technologies born of the Industrial Revolution in Europe and America, settlers believed that a railroad could conquer the great Outback. Brimming with enthusiasm and indifferent to the challenges of nature in the barren land, European engineers set about laying track northward from Adelaide, with visions of opening up vast new areas for farming, trade, and general settlement. The railway builders succeeded in reaching Alice Springs with narrow-gauge rails and steam engines. But the railroad never became the reliable transportation system its proponents had imagined. Weather and the vagaries of Outback terrain plagued and perplexed the line. Dust storms often delayed or halted trains. Sporadic flash floods washed away sections of the line, compelling the builders to spend as much time repairing the tracks as running the trains. Not until 1980, when the rail line was relaid on a more stable path with modern materials, did the railway achieve reliability.

When their scheme of an Outback railway was largely defeated by nature, enterprising European settlers turned to a more prudent, if primitive,

Opposite:

A yellow-footed rock-wallaby pauses long enough to be photographed in the Flinders Ranges north of Adelaide. Smaller cousins of the kangaroo, rock-wallabies developed specialized features for life on steep slopes. Their rigid tails serve as stabilizing poles as they jump about rock outcroppings, and studs on the soles of their hind feet provide secure footing.

means of transporting the trappings of civilization into an empty realm. They used camels. As early as 1840, camels were imported as desert beasts of burden. For decades, linked together in long trains and driven by Afghan handlers, these creatures pulled countless wagonloads of supplies and building materials into the Australian interior, naturally coping with desert conditions in a way the mightiest machines of humanity could not.

The wagon trains are gone, but the descendants of the earliest camels remain. Turned free when their usefulness declined, camels became a new feature of the Outback, roaming in wild herds that survive today. Estimates of the number of wild camels at liberty in the outback reach as high as 30,000. In fact, Australia's feral camel herds are now the only wild camels left in the world, and in an ironic reversal, are now often exported to the Middle East.

On the outskirts of Alice Springs, the Cousteau team found an enduring symbol of earlier times, a camel farm and tourist attraction operated by breeder Noel Fullerton, whose flowing white beard and desert-weathered visage have appeared along with the famous face of golfer Greg Norman in international tourism ads for Australia. Fullerton has been raising and riding camels since the 1950s, when there were few roads around Alice Springs and locals often kept four camels—a buggy camel, a riding camel, a wagon camel, and a pack camel.

Fullerton spent a day sharing his camel knowledge and experiences with our team. Recalling the old days, he extolled the virtues of his animals to Chapman and Wilcox. "Our areas out here were fourteen or fifteen days between water," he said. "Whereas a horse has to drink every day, these fellas can go up to thirty days without a drink."

Fullerton told them that camels had been treated unfairly by writers who dwell on their stubbornness and their disagreeable habit of spitting at handlers. "I reckon camels have got a bad name," he said, "but they don't deserve it. They opened up a lot of country. And the camel is a gentle animal if he's treated right. Moreover, they last a goodly time, even out here. They live up to forty-eight years as an average, so they're not only reliable but they're around for a long while."

Fullerton asked if one of the team members wanted to try riding a camel. Silence. The old camel hand laughed and offered to pick a likely candidate. Soon Wilcox, who had the misfortune of standing next to Fullerton, was being led into a corral and introduced to his mount. The lack of enthusiasm seemed mutual. Wilcox climbed aboard as a farmhand tried to coax the camel to its feet, a campaign that proved difficult and time-consuming.

When at last the camel rose, Wilcox bounced off on a trotting animal whose bulbous back seemed to shift about in unpredictable and uncomfort-

Equipped with a specialized digestive system that detoxifies the poisons contained in certain kinds of eucalypt leaves, the koala ensures itself a food supply - that is unpalatable to most other animals. The marsupial also possesses strong jaws and teeth to grind down the tough eucalypt leaves. Though some 700 species of eucalypts, or gum trees, are found in Australia, koalas feed mostly on only about fourteen varieties of eucalypts. Despite its popular characterization as a koala "bear," the mammal is unrelated to the bear family, but is a distant relative of the possums. Though generally solitary and lethargic, koalas are capable of violent confrontations during courtship, when males attack one another with teeth and claws, and the act of reproduction is marked by a loud and furious struggle between the tree-bound pairs.

Camels and riders compete in the world-renowned Camel Cup Races held each May at Alice Springs. For residents of the interior, and tourists who flock here from throughout the country, the Camel Cup is the Outback equivalent of classic thoroughbred horse races in Europe and America.

able ways. The team watched with a mix of amusement and foreboding. This was the same Clay Wilcox whose undersea exploits had resulted in a score of minor injuries—including a leg bruised by the powerful fin of a humpback whale, a hand painfully shocked by an electric ray, and buttocks nipped by playful sea lions. Though jarred and humbled, Wilcox brought a certain amount of honor to the sailors and divers rooting for him by concluding his half-hour camel ride unharmed.

For many in the Outback, however, camel riding is not just a source of tourist fees but a rollicking sport. As it happened, our team was in Alice Springs for the Outback equivalent of the Irish Sweepstakes or the Kentucky Derby—an annual extravaganza called the Camel Cup Carnival. Run on a Saturday each May, the event draws cameleers from hundreds of miles away, as well as media crews, bagpipe bands, racing enthusiasts, and tourists who seemed uncertain whether to laugh or cheer as the ungainly camels spit in disdain at their jockeys, then gallop inelegantly, and to a large degree independently, around a dirt oval track. Yet the sport is taken seriously by its participants and boasts its share of luminaries, though the team had the impression that for many riders the thrill of victory may have been surpassed by the pleasure of simply knowing that the agony of the ride was finally over. Most importantly, as Anne-Marie observed, the races seemed a celebration of the individualistic, offbeat character of life in the Outback, and the camels themselves served as hardy and cantankerous symbols of that life.

Near Alice Springs, Noel Fullerton breeds, raises, and races camels in the Outback. Originally imported as beasts of burden in the treacherous interior, camels serve today largely as tourist attractions. Some 30,000 wild camels, descendants of early domestic herds, roam freely across vast stretches of the bush.

Our deeper interest in the world of the Red Center, however, lay beyond the paved streets and frontier ambience of Alice Springs. For several weeks our

Antoine Rosset studies Aboriginal rock art that is among the earliest known expressions of human creativity. Similar paintings found in north Australia may be 35,000 years old. Dugong drawings in this coastal cave suggest that early Aboriginals hunted the huge marine mammals.

land team roamed the rutted roads that strike out from the town toward distant, often temporary encampments, roads that carry a sprinkling of curious outsiders each year beyond the bounds of modern civilization to the periphery of the human past. Though most of Australia's 200,000 remaining Aboriginals (about a quarter of whom are of unmixed descent) live in native settlements or modern towns, some endure as nomadic holdouts from the present, moving steadily about the desert along routes that wind among natural landmarks cherished across the millenia.

Long ridiculed as a backward, squalid people by the white immigrants who gained dominion over the continent, Aboriginals have only recently been elevated legally in Australia and recognized as heirs to an ancient, accomplished, and complex culture. (We use the word Aboriginals, pre-

Common to ancient Aboriginal art are figures portraying the mythical ancestors of the Dreamtime, an ill-defined time in the past when beings in the form of humans, animals, and plants roamed the land, fashioning its natural features. For Aboriginals, the Dreamtime continues as a kind of other side of life, in which the destiny of all things is determined.

ferred by the indigenous people we met, rather than the more commonly employed Aborigines.) Our interest lay in understanding how Aboriginals had managed to flourish in a hostile environment that defeated most of the Europeans who undertook to explore and tame it. Time and again white expeditions into the great desert met with disaster as men and horses succumbed to hunger, thirst, heat, scurvy, venomous animals and plants, and accidents inflicted by the rugged terrain.

Yet in amazing contrast, Aboriginal peoples have lived successfully in the same harsh realm across 50,000 years, making theirs perhaps the oldest surviving culture on earth. This extraordinary persistence has been achieved by thousands of generations who developed no wheels, no metal, no pottery, no fabrics, no domesticated animals, no agriculture, no written language, and no permanent dwellings. What great secret, we wondered, enabled Aboriginals to succeed where waves of European pioneers wielding every advantage of modern civilization had largely failed?

During our travels about the Red Center, we met Diana and Greg Snowden-James, two white Australians who had spent years working on Aboriginal reserves as teachers and counselors. With two members of the Pitjantjatjara people, Nganyinytja (who conceived the project) and her husband, Ilyatjari, they had organized small-scale trips in which tourists with a serious interest in traditional culture could spend a week living the indigenous life-style in an Aboriginal encampment. It was Nganyinytja's conviction that Australian urban dwellers would understand Aboriginal needs better if there were a way to bring the two cultures together in a traditional Aboriginal setting. The Snowden-Jameses and Nganyinytja's group of Pitjantjatjaras consented to allow our land team to join one of these educational encounters and to document Aboriginal methods of survival in the Australian interior.

We joined the Pitjantjatjara at an encampment named Angatja, nearly 300 miles southwest of Alice Springs at the end of a dirt track that branches off a lonely desert road called Gunbarrel Highway. For the next ten days, we lived generally as hunters and gatherers, or at least as hunters and gatherers equipped with cameras and sound recorders.

The Pitjantjatjara have ranged for thousands of years across a well-defined tract of the desert southwest of present-day Alice Springs that covers about 30,000 square miles. They are one of an estimated 500 to 600 Aboriginal tribal associations that once existed in Australia, descendants of people who came to the continent from Southeast Asia by way of Indonesia. Their forebears, while of uncertain origin, became the first-known navigators as they sailed across sea lanes separating Australia from Asia, and they are credited with several other archaeological firsts, including the most ancient evidence of human cremation and of edge-ground stone ax heads.

While many Aboriginal peoples settled along tropical coastlines to the north and in the colder regions as far south as Tasmania, the ancestors of the Pitjantjatjara evidently adopted the hot central desert as a homeland. They devised ways of surviving in an environment that, today, yields no permanent streams and receives an average rainfall less than the rate of evaporation. The search for food and water in this difficult world forced the Pitjantjatjara to adopt a life of wide-ranging mobility.

Yet a nomadic existence alone, we conjectured, could not fully explain how humanity found sufficient water to endure the baking sun day after day across thousands of years. In one of their first lessons, a group of elders took me to a gum tree that rose from flat, dusty, seemingly waterless land. Using a sharp branch as a tool, they dug for fifteen minutes, cut off a two-foot length of tree root, passed it to me, and, with broad smiles, indicated through hand gestures that I should hold it above my head. A trickle of cool water dripped into my upturned mouth, only a few spoonfuls of moisture, but enough to ease thirst and to sustain life. Little was wasted as the Pitjantjatjara gingerly passed the root section from person to person. I recalled the words of our Cousteau biologist Dr. Richard Murphy, who has traveled widely among indigenous peoples during our expeditions: "Where water is abundant, its importance is forgotten. Where it is scarce, even a few drops are treasured."

Through time, Aboriginals compiled an oral catalog of every place in the vast desert where even a few drops of water might be hidden—sheltered rock-hole catchments, creek bed soakages where deep water remained after a heavy flood, widely scattered but oozing springs, the forks of large gum trees, the roots of certain trees, and, when there was no other source, the bodily water of hibernating frogs, or even the morning dew. In sandy or clay

Jean-Michel Cousteau samples water from the root of a gum tree. Aboriginals displayed their skill in finding water in the arid Outback for the Cousteau team.

areas, Aboriginals looked for certain small herbs found only where groundwater is close to the surface. Here they dug a well, which sometimes provided a reliable source of water for a long period of time, but more often dried up after a few weeks.

In like manner, as we learned from the Pitjantjatjara, Aboriginals gained across the millennia an encyclopedic knowledge of every possible desert source of food. As with most ancient cultures, men were primarily the hunters, women the gatherers. Following Nganyinytja and other women day by day, we saw that Aboriginal women led a more arduous life than men and provided a larger portion of the daily food supply. While responsible for gathering plant foods and smaller animals, a time-consuming task, they also prepared and cooked the food, fetched firewood and water, helped build the family hut or windbreak—all the while taking the major responsibility for child care as well. This relentless routine could involve walking twenty miles a day to find food, digging laboriously, and carrying heavy water containers. And all of this hard physical work often was carried out in the sun in temperatures well above one hundred degrees Fahrenheit. To us, the most remarkable feat of all was the uncomplaining, cheerful manner in which all of these exhaustive tasks were accomplished.

We saw as well that despite the apparent barrenness of the terrain, the women gathered a constant diet of nutritious foods. Anthropologists have estimated that Aboriginals use at least 300 different desert plants alone as food. The menus we confronted were not *our* notion of inviting fare, and we often joined their meals with a discomfort that amused them. We could only assume that the Pitjantjatjara would no doubt have faced a Parisian offering of cassoulet or bouillabaisse with similar queasiness.

The Aboriginal equivalent of bread came from grass-seed pods ground with water into a paste, which was shaped into a lump and cooked for about twenty minutes in fire ashes, creating a hard but healthy cake. The women also gathered and prepared fruits and berries, yams, roots, snails, bird and reptile eggs, burrowing rodents, lizards, and snakes. Two foods prized by the Pitjantjatjara seem the most difficult for outsiders to appreciate. Foremost are grubs, larvae of a desert beetle, which infest the roots of a common plant called the witchetty bush. Though we all sampled witchetty grubs, which are eaten raw or lightly cooked, we did so without the enthusiasm of Aboriginal children, for whom their nutlike flavor may offer a pleasure similar to that of peanut butter elsewhere. Regardless of one's subjective appreciation of grubs as snacks, however, the larvae are rich in calories, protein, and fat. According to UNESCO, ten large grubs are sufficient to provide the daily nutritional needs of an adult.

One morning, to the delight of their children, the women led us to a site

A Pitjantjatjara woman shares honey ants with Diana Snowden-James and her son. The Snowden-Jameses help the tribe operate a small-scale tourist operation permitting outsiders to learn traditional survival techniques by living with the Aboriginals for a week at a time.

away from camp where they dug into the ground and uncovered a nest of ants. It was as if they had opened a candy jar. The insects are called honey ants, and for Aboriginals they have long served as a confection of nature.

In the honey ant colony, certain workers are used as storage vessels, accumulating in their bellies a sugary food gathered by other workers from the sap of the mulga tree. The abdomens of these living containers swell up into balloonlike beads of sweetness, leaving the creatures too bloated even to walk. When times are tough, the entire ant colony draws sustenance from their immobile corps of honey pots.

A Pitjantjatjara woman withdrew a few plump honey ants from the hole and demonstrated how to suck the sweetness from the abdominal bubble of a living ant. Despite the disagreeableness of the act, and the minute portion provided by a single ant, the team had to agree that the taste was as pleasant as the more conventional candies served up by other cultures.

Traditionally, while tribal women carried out their daily routines, the men hunted or made tools. The detailed knowledge of desert plants and small animals among women was mirrored by the intimate understanding among men of how to find and capture the wary prey of the desert. They perfected techniques of tracking their prey by reading faint markings on the ground, broken twigs, bent grasses, or displaced stones. Moreover, they studied the seasonal movements of their quarry like scientists.

Though Aboriginals never developed bows and arrows, they used spears with unparalleled skill, and supplemented this primary weapon with

Certain worker honey ants accumulate sugary food in their abdomens, serving the colony as living storage containers. The Pitjantjatjara consider the nectar a delicacy and taught the Cousteau team how to get it.

boomerangs, clubs, traps, and snares. Kangaroos, wallabies, possums, giant lizards, ostrichlike emus, and snakes were speared. Clubs and boomerangs were thrown into bird flocks, stunning or killing a few birds, driving others into hidden nets.

At some point during their 50,000-year residence in Australia, Aboriginals began to employ another tool in their hunts. The long grasses that shoot up across the desert following rains were probably an obstacle to good hunting. They made travel difficult, for one thing, and perhaps more importantly, they concealed not only prey but venomous snakes, which Aboriginals understandably dreaded. Sporadic lightning fires, however, cleared the grasses, making both dangerous snakes and prey such as wallabies easier to detect. Fires were also followed during wet seasons by a flush of new growth, which attracted kangaroos and wallabies like a kind of bait. Perhaps inspired by these blessings of accidental fire, Aboriginals began to use systematic burnings to enhance their environment. Across tens of thousands of years, widespread use of fire gradually changed the landscape of inland Australia. Fire-resistant plants prospered and replaced those vulnerable to burnings; other plants evolved adaptations to fire. A kind of bush called heartleaf became dependent on the right kind of fires—not too hot and about seven years apart. As such fires spread through thickets, the heat cracked heartleaf seed cases and allowed them to germinate.

As plant life changed, so too did the animal life that fed upon it, and the subtle wisdom of Aboriginal management resulted in conditions that favored those creatures upon which the tribes depended for meat. So pervasive was Aboriginal use of fire ecology across the ages, and so pronounced were its effects, that scientists today credit ancient tribes with virtually creating the flora and fauna in vast parts of the Australian continent.

Our stay with the Pitjantjatjara gave us a brief but profound sense of life in the bush, and an appreciation of the intelligence, strength, and spiritual depth of Aboriginal peoples. To the degree that it is possible for humans raised in an industrial world to comprehend the feelings and ethics of people whose lives are still largely at the mercy of nature, we felt a genuine kinship with the families who welcomed us into their ancient way of life.

Perhaps bemused by our gear and our unfamiliarity with things they take for granted, they instructed us patiently and seemed to proffer their friendship easily. In traditional manner, they characterized each of us with a nickname, demonstrating in the process their persistent and lively sense of humor. Perhaps inspired by my beard, they named me after the lizard known as the thorny devil. Philippe Morice, who had replaced Deloire as our cameraman and impressed the tribe with his agility as he climbed rocks for unusual camera angles, was called Mountain Kangaroo. Wilcox, tall and blond, was dubbed White Owl. Inexplicably, sound engineer Holland became Boomerang, Chapman was named Emu, and Jackson took the name Big Lizard. Whether because of her unflagging curiosity or her striking role as the only woman on our team, the Pitjantjatjara seemed especially taken by Anne-Marie, whom they treated with an extra measure of warmth and attention. They sought her out first when there was a new food to share or a wonder of the desert environment to explain. Perhaps their special affection for Anne-Marie was most evident in the name they bestowed upon her. For the length of our stay, she was called Honey Ant.

Yet despite the easy relationships we enjoyed with the Pitjantjatjara, it was difficult to bridge the great cultural gap between our Western world view and theirs, which is ever linked to a concept called the Dreamtime, or the Dreaming. The more we learned about this religious thread through their lives—by reading anthropological studies and by talking with the Snowden-Jameses and the Pitjantjatjaras—the more we realized how integral it was not only to their buoyant character as a people but to their extraordinary success in turning the hostile environment into a source of sustenance, into a comfortable home.

Aboriginals believe that the world was created during the Dreamtime—an ill-defined period in the past—by ancestral beings who were part human, part animal, and who roamed the land turning it from an empty plain into the desert forms that surround them. Individual features of the terrain are associated with mythic events. A meandering creek bed may have been created by an ancestral snake. A boulder may be the petrified eggs of a great Dreamtime bird-human. As Aboriginals range about the Outback, they see in the configurations of the land a habitat laid out for them by superhuman heroes, as parents might create a giant playground for generations to come, filled not only with things of wonder but the means by which to sustain life forever.

But while the creation of the world happened in the past, the Dreamtime has no clear ending. The heroes turned into many of the natural features of the land and their spiritual essences are still alive in such places as rock outcroppings and waterholes and caves, from which they still control the machinery of continued existence. The Dreamtime, then, also embodies the present and future, a kind of "everywhen," a kind of other side of life. A graphic explanation of the concept was once offered by an elderly Aboriginal who watched a DC-3 aircraft land on a desert strip. At the old man's side was a visiting anthropologist, who was trying to understand the Dreamtime. The man pointed to the whirling propellers of the airplane. When the "swinging sticks" were stopped, the Aboriginal observed, one could not see through them. That was like the present, like the Aboriginals alive today. When the propellers were spinning, one could see through them. That was like the Dreamtime, the other dimension of life.

There are both totemic and, curiously, musical components to this belief. As the Dreamtime beings traveled about they sang out the names of everything they created—animals, plants, rocks, hills—leaving a trail of songs describing natural features. Each living Aboriginal is today linked to one of these ancient beings, and takes as a totem the kind of animal represented by the hero. A man might be an Emu, his wife a Wallaby, one of his children a Carpet Snake, another a Brush Turkey. Each inherits a particular "songline" created by the totemic ancestor, which contains an invisible and unique pathway across the desert. An Aboriginal can go "walkabout," following their memorized musical map on a ritual journey in the footprints of his or her personal Dreamtime ancestor. The great arid expanse marked by table rock and spinifex grass and dry riverbeds was to Aboriginals a sacred frozen music. Their role in this timeless symphony was to appreciate it and, by living according to its laws, simply to exist. Aboriginals do not see themselves as superior to other elements or beings of nature, but as key factors in maintaining a harmony among nature's component parts. As a result of their spiritual connections to the land, we concluded, they were perhaps the world's first ecologists.

Accordingly, living among elements of nature created by the ancients and still inhabited by them, connected personally to specific animal totems, Aboriginals walk across their land in reverence. The land is now and always has been as the Dreamtime heroes sang it into being, as they meant it to be. It is not territory that can be bought or sold or in any way possessed, nor is it an undeveloped wasteland to be improved. It is perfect as it is and should not be changed.

It seemed to us, as the Pitjantjatjara led us to stones and caves linked to Dreamtime stories, that their reverence toward the land was similar to that of a Westerner who enters a famous cathedral. To most of us, desecration of a revered religious site would be unthinkable, and to the Aboriginal the notion of altering the landscape is similarly abhorrent. Thus, despite the longevity of their culture, Aboriginal impact on the environment has been limited to their careful burning of grasslands, to such temporary changes as digging wells or cutting down trees for tools, and to cave paintings, among the oldest on earth, in which Dreamtime stories were recorded as art.

Because they built no pyramids, temples, cities, aqueducts, roads, bridges, vehicles, or skyscrapers; because their tool kits did not grow beyond devices of wood and stone; because none of their 300 languages

A Pitjantjatjara woman dons traditional makeup for ceremonies marking the end of a week spent with white visitors. As part of their learning experience, guests join in festive dancing around an evening campfire.

were ever written; because they did not refashion the landscape with vast programs of agriculture or forestry or mining, Aboriginals are still regarded widely as primitive and simple people to the outside world. Yet many of the civilizations that we deem advanced destroyed the very fabric of nature that supported them. Most flourished during an age of glory and then disappeared, while the Aboriginals of Australia endured. To us, the fact that this ancient desert culture still exists is proof that it must have qualities worthy of our study and perhaps even emulation.

Because Aboriginal culture remained isolated for tens of thousands of years, and its belief system went unchallenged from generation to generation, it remains today a nearly unshakable foundation of desert life. The Pitjantjatjara, for example, have adopted many Western technologies, but these devices tend to be ones that enhance the traditional way of life, not products that greatly alter it. Thus, they have made nomadic travel easier by using trucks. They communicate with other tribes and families in the distance using two-way radios, enabling them, for example, to organize ritual gatherings in a few hours that once took weeks. They hunt with rifles, often use tents instead of traditional shelters, cook with metal pots. But it seemed to us that they carefully reject all but those technologies that improve, even strengthen, the old ways.

On our last night with the Pitjantjatjara, we were treated to exuberant singing and dancing around a roaring campfire. We tried, unsuccessfully for the most part, to play their traditional instruments, like the drone pipe called a *didjeridoo*. Some of us joined their dances, eliciting polite but animated laughter. Watching, I thought about the kindness and generosity of these new friends, saw in their faces and movements a grace and handsomeness usually overlooked by outsiders, and saw as well the beauty of their world. The desert seemed to flow away in every direction toward infinity. The air was so crystal clear that I could see the face of the moon in extraordinary detail.

In her journal that night, Anne-Marie wrote:

"Tonight I understood. Being with the Pitjantjatjaras and listening to their mythical stories in the night—the most beautiful night sky I've ever seen, so full of stars above the immensity of the desert—you begin to understand, very deeply within yourself, what the Aboriginals mean by the Dreamtime. As you listen to the stories, you begin to realize that the Dreamtime is still today. We saw the Aboriginals rub the rocks out in the bush so that the Dreamtime would stay with them.

"We are brought up in a Western world. We don't go out in the bush and live. But when you're there, being with those people all the time and listening to their stories, you begin to see the world as they do."

For a Pitjantjatjara man, the mix of traditional and contemporary means incorporating into his dance costume not only grasses and body painting but sneakers, shorts, and a floor mop.

121

After bidding farewell to the Snowden-Jameses and the Pitjantjatjara at Angatja, we drove to a place that is sacrosanct to most Aboriginals. Some 200 miles southwest of Alice Springs, at the eastern edge of the Pitjantjatjara's traditional range, we could see in the distance a gargantuan red rock embedded not only in the vacant desert but in the very heart of Aboriginal culture.

We were not alone in this undertaking. Buses loaded with tourists lined the road, as if carrying pilgrims to a strange kind of Mecca. Like us, vacationers were drawn to a site that is not only starkly beautiful but is, from an Aboriginal perspective, the most spectacular feature created by the Dreamtime beings in the whole of Australia.

The Aboriginals call it *Uluru*. In 1870, European explorers named it Ayers Rock after then South Australian Premier Henry Ayers, and the Aboriginal name was discarded by white Australia until recently. In 1985, to quell a growing dispute, the area was deeded to the Pitjantjatjaras and the Yankunytjatjara, who together call themselves the Anangu. The tribes in turn leased the rock and surrounding land back to the government to be administered as a national park. Since then, the name Uluru has appeared alongside Ayers Rock on maps.

Uluru is a single rock, a sandstone monolith. More than 3.5 miles of rock are believed to be hidden beneath the flat plain from which its weathered crest rises well over a thousand feet. Like other formations we had encountered in the outback and Kimberleys, it was formed 600 million years ago as part of the sea, hardened by the ages and eventually tilted upward, to be worn and pitted by the searing heat, winds, and thunderstorms across a hundred thousand million days. Although the interior of the rock is grey, the iron content in the outer skin has oxidized over the years — in other words, rusted — to turn the huge landmark a shade of red that is heightened in intensity by the desert sun and air, and further dramatized by its midday contrast with the vivid blue of the desert sky.

Most of Uluru is off-limits to all but Aboriginals, for whom the rock serves as a kind of bible. Every crevice, furrowed depression, and cave can be read by Aboriginals like verses of scripture to reveal a Dreamtime meaning. Along the western side of the rock, however, tourists are permitted to climb along a low railing to the summit. While we filmed, Wilcox and Chapman joined the few hardy tourists attempting the steep, exhausting ascent. Though the air seemed dead still along the base of Uluru, Wilcox and Chapman found a stiff wind roaring about the top. Rangers told them the climb could be deceptively dangerous. More than a dozen people had died trying to catch windblown hats and other items. In the process, they lost balance and fell, unimpeded by Uluru's smooth slopes, to their deaths.

Reaching the top, Wilcox and Chapman gazed out upon a kind of earthy emptiness that stretched to the horizon in every direction, broken only by another lumpy, orange-colored collection of monoliths twenty miles to the west called Kata Tjuta (the Olgas). While instructive of the unending flatness of the surrounding desert floor, the view did not seem adequate compensation for the agony of the climb. Chapman recalled the words of a Scottish explorer named David Carnegie, who led a small party near this region in 1896. "Words can give no conception," he wrote in his journal, "of the ghastly desolation and hopeless dreariness of the scene which meets one's eyes from the crest of a high ridge."

Today, nearly 300,000 tourists come each year to behold Uluru. It struck us as a curious irony that many who now trek to this sacred Aboriginal site are probably descended from early Australian settlers who ruthlessly exploited Aboriginals and even attempted to exterminate them. Sometimes they succeeded. In Tasmania, where Aboriginals were often hunted like wild game, the last full-blooded native died in 1905. European settlement brought not only massacres and enslavement, but diseases that raged through the indigenous population. Smallpox, venereal disease, tuberculosis, whooping cough, measles, leprosy, and influenza ravaged Aboriginal tribes, reducing an estimated original population of 300,000 to about 40,000 in the 1930s, and completely eradicating some groups.

Over the years, more than 350 separate Aboriginal reserves were created by Australian authorities, where most natives were resettled in makeshift towns, a program by which they could be controlled, converted to Christianity, and educated in the language and laws of the governing majority. During a *Calypso* land team expedition along the Cape York Peninsula, and also while *Alcyone*'s land team traveled inland from the coast of Western Australia, we had visited some of these Aboriginal reserves. Mostly, they seemed places of despair, where social workers tried valiantly to improve Aboriginal life, but where the native peoples had been isolated from the ways of life and belief they still craved. Their sustenance came from welfare, their escape from alcohol. Descended from a culture that gave little value to material possessions, they acquired modern gadgets but discarded them like garbage. Rusting cars were strewn about the reserve towns, abandoned wherever they were wrecked by drunken drivers. Many Aboriginals, a disproportionate number it seemed to us, end up in jail, in part because of alcohol-related incidents, in part because of alleged discrimination in the application of the laws, in part because of ignorance of legal rights. Young Aboriginals often flee authorities, fearful of police prejudice and brutality.

Largely without modern educations, Aboriginals have trouble finding

Overleaf:
Tourists follow a steep path to the top of Ayers Rock, known to Aboriginals as Uluru and considered perhaps the most sacred site in Australia to the indigenous people. In 1985, as the result of Aboriginal protests, the government deeded the monolith and surrounding lands to Aboriginals, who leased the rock back as Uluru National Park. The rock is now one of the country's most popular tourist destinations.

jobs, but not the beer they call grog—which further dislocates a noble culture and deepens the Aboriginal's sense of being lost in time. The despair over alcohol pervaded a town we visited in Western Australia. We filmed a town meeting among elders of the Bardi tribe, where angry arguments broke out as the community leaders wrestled with a seemingly hopeless problem.

Returning to Alice Springs, however, we found a measure of future hope for the Aboriginal peoples. We were shown video tapes of a protest march by Aboriginal women through the streets of Alice Springs. In traditional dress, these mothers, wives, and daughters confronted local authorities and implored them to halt widespread sale of alcohol on Aboriginal lands.

The event was symbolic of the new surge of Aboriginal concern for their fading culture, and of their increasing attempts to achieve political reforms that will ensure respect for their past and a rebirth of their life-styles. One campaign involves dismantling the settlements imposed by white Australia so that Aboriginals can return to their own country and re-establish their traditional groups. The Australian government has taken steps during the last twenty years to accommodate this desire in parts of the country, transferring tens of millions of acres of Aboriginal reserve lands to Aboriginal ownership under Land Trusts. Accordingly, widespread movements from reserves to small outstation camps like Angatja have taken place in parts of the Western desert. For some Aboriginals, whose lives are now irrevocably tied to the modern world, it seems impossible entirely to re-enter the old ways. Their solution is to spend the weekends camping in the Outback, reliving the ancient life in increments, teaching their children traditional knowledge and beliefs on family excursions.

In Alice Springs we met an Aboriginal woman named Freda Glynn, who is spearheading a novel project meant to support the renewal of traditional ways using present-day technology. Glynn has raised enough money to establish an Aboriginal radio and television station. Her goal is to help elevate the self-respect of Aboriginals, who often suffer from a lack of attention by the existing media. Through her efforts, distant tribes in the bush can now tune in to FM and short-wave radio broadcasts which disperse Aboriginal news exclusively, as well as educational programs designed to increase literacy in English while at the same time reinforcing native languages. Though her television station reaches a limited audience, Glynn also produces inspirational and educational video tapes for distribution to Aboriginal schools.

"We have contemporary rock-and-roll songs about health," she told us, "and about historical and political decisions the government's taken, about AIDS, about beating the grog and what alcohol does to you, how it wrecks

your family. And we're using music and the radio in a different kind of way as direct education. It's really important for self-esteem and pride that Aboriginal people can see their own culture up on television and on radio the same as the dominant culture."

One problem faced by those Aboriginals who seek to live the traditional life-style is basic economics. Even the most remote groups have become somewhat dependent on Western products, and are thus obliged to acquire the money needed to purchase them. Fortunately, the upsurge in Australian awareness of the Aboriginal culture has spawned an appreciation of their ancient arts and crafts. Today, in Alice Springs and throughout the country, art galleries and tourist gift shops do a lively business in the sale of

Some Aboriginals believe that the creation of the world during the Dreamtime began at Uluru. For them, every crevice and cave of the great sandstone monolith—a single rock—bears Dreamtime meanings and stories, like the verses of an immense stone bible.

Aboriginal art, not only their highly stylized oil and watercolor paintings, but baskets, bags, wood carvings, jewelry, and leather goods. Young Aboriginal musicians have even succeeded in combining traditional music with modern rock, a hybrid form that has gained great popularity recently and elevated some bands to national prominence.

As interest in Australia itself has escalated internationally in recent years, admiration of Aboriginal artwork has spread around the world. As a result, many Aboriginal artists and tribes now earn sufficient fees from their traditional arts and crafts to support their return to the land. Perhaps most importantly, the surge in appreciation of Aboriginal culture has increased the perception among most Australians that the "First Australians" represent an invaluable national source of pride, and that preservation of their society and their sacred sites can enrich the entire country.

When our land team mission through the Outback came to an end, I recounted our experiences to Cousteau Society biologist Dick Murphy, who had himself spent a great deal of time reflecting on Aboriginal culture as a result of contacts with tribes in Western Australia. Murphy has written papers analyzing the ecological impact of indigenous peoples and that intangible aspect of culture which we simplistically refer to as "happiness." It is his opinion that the quotient of contentment and fulfillment, as well as ecological understanding, is often greater among native peoples than among those of us blessed with the amenities of modern civilization. Though recognizing that it is impossible to refashion the world, he laments the comparative stress, consumption of resources, insecurity, impact on the biosphere, and frenetic pace our industrialized society has created.

Murphy believes that the roots of many modern problems trace back to the differing mentality that developed between ancient hunter-gatherers and the pastoralists and farmers who initiated so-called modern societies. "In contrast to a hunter-gatherer," he told me, "a pastoralist, for example, nurtures and controls an animal species solely to harvest food and fiber for himself. The life of the sheep or goat or cow is considered only in the context of its value to humans.

"History has shown that it is not a great leap to extend such hierarchical thinking, such a mentality of control and exploitation, to other races, cultures, and religions. The resulting prejudices become deeply embedded in our cultures, leading to obvious conflicts. But exercising such control— whether it be over crops, herds, or people—requires a lot of work. Thus civilizations based on exploitation and dominance hold a work ethic in high regard."

Murphy smiled. "And what would be the predictable view in such a

society of nomads who believe humankind is no better than rocks, wombats, or weather; of hunter-gatherers who construct nothing, possess almost nothing, and go through life naked? Yet if you look at the situation from another angle, our 'civilized' approach to the world seldom takes into account the quality of life, a sense of place and belonging, feelings of contentment and inner peace, and an ethic of equality and unity of all things. Were one to judge Aboriginal society wholly on these latter qualities, it might be superior to our own.

"At the dawn of civilization, the differences between husbanding animals and gathering berries might have seemed minute, but the implications may have been enormous across time. Can we say that one strategy or mentality was better than the other? Probably not. But I find it interesting to project each of these two approaches into the future, imagining what the consequences of each means to the vitality of the planet and the quality of human life. We can't all start wandering the desert gathering seed pods for bread, but perhaps we can find ways to learn from the Aboriginals about our place in nature, and about the values of regarding the natural world that sustains and exalts us not with disdain but with reverence."

In our experiences with the Pitjantjatjara and other Aboriginal peoples, in our gradual comprehension not only of the hardships of life in the great desert but its rewards and its beauty, and now in Murphy's words, I had found the answer to my original question: how could a people nearly devoid of the advantages of modern civilization have survived so long in a realm that defeated most of the white explorers and settlers who entered it?

The answer was obvious. The Aboriginals conquered the desert by becoming part of it.

AFTER THE FLOOD OF INVADERS

Drifting along in the regimens of sustenance and the rituals of Dreamtime, generations of Aboriginals saw the sun rise over Australia nearly twenty million times before new invaders arrived to challenge their stoic reign. Elsewhere, more aggressive societies had arisen, and these distant kingdoms were curious to acquire whatever riches lay beyond their home shores. The existence of a great southern continent had been theorized since medieval times. Were there not such a huge land mass to the south, reasoned ancient geographers, the world would tip over. European explorers set out to find it.

In fact, there is some evidence that merchant seamen from China may have been the first non-Aboriginals to visit Australia, but their experiences are lost to history. In the 17th century, seven navigators (six Dutch and one English) landed at scattered points along the north and west coasts of the mainland and in Tasmania. Generally, they pronounced the land unfit for human habitation and departed for more appealing places.

Australia became a distant outpost of the British Empire rather than of some other colonial power only because the more promising reports of Captain James Cook, who explored the eastern coast in 1770, convinced English authorities to found a settlement there. Yet such a strange and far country was not a fitting locale for lords and ladies. The British chose to use Australia as a colossal natural prison. In January of 1788, eleven small ships of the famous First Fleet arrived from Portsmouth with 1,382 people—about half of them male and female convicts, about half seamen, soldiers, wives, and children. They established a penal colony at Sydney Cove and became the first European residents of Australia.

As decades passed, penal colonies gave way to conventional settlements, and the image of the southern continent gradually changed from a far-removed holding cell to a frontier that might someday yield mineral or even agricultural wealth to hardy souls. European immigrants struck out for Australia—and emancipated convicts migrated inland—not to settle harmoniously into its challenging environment but to tame it with technology. The terrain was not for them a masterpiece created by superhuman ancient heroes but a virgin resource to be exploited for profit. Europeans, after all, were heroic themselves: builders of great ships, navigators of vast oceans, inventors of cannons and telescopes and whale-oil lamps, heirs to the intellectual glories of Greece, Rome, and the Renaissance. They had gained dominion over their original homelands, built canals and castles, turned woodlands into farmlands, cultivated a pastoral beauty framed by

White man got no Dreaming.
Him go 'nother way . . .
Him got road belong himself.

•

A Gagudju man, quoted by
writer Stanley Breeden

Dams on the River Murray provided an abundant new source of dependable water for agriculture, turning once barren lands into nearly two million acres of orchards and vegetable fields that comprise Australia's most important food-production center. But dams also have blocked fish migrations and disrupted other vital processes of the river.

Regarded as harmless storybook creatures elsewhere, rabbits are symbols of destruction in Australia. Imported and released to the wild by a homesick English immigrant in 1859, twenty-four rabbits flourished in an ecosystem devoid of natural enemies, growing within sixty years into a rabbit plague that spread across half of the continent, devouring native vegetation and displacing indigenous animals. Today, rabbits remain a dramatic illustration of the hazards of introducing foreign species into a delicately balanced and fragile environment.

hedgerows and haystacks and tree-lined post roads. What they left behind fit their accepted definition of natural beauty. Though some explorers and early pioneers found promise in the dry continent of Australia, they did not by and large see much beauty there. But with ambition and hard work, they would remake the ugly land into something resembling the beautiful countrysides they recalled.

The problem was: Australia was not Europe. Technologies and agricultural schemes that succeeded in the rich soils, predictable seasons, and plentiful precipitation of the old country did not always work in the arid southern continent. Before Europeans arrived, there had never been a hoofed animal in Australia. Within a century of settlement, there were hundreds of millions of sheep and cattle. The pasture lands of Europe could support such creatures, but the fragile soils and grasses of Australia were nearly trampled into wastelands in many areas.

The chaotic effects of importing alien animals into the highly specialized, delicately balanced Australian ecosystem surprised and perplexed early settlers, and spawned troubles that endure today. No story so dramatically illustrates the problem as the textbook case of European rabbits.

Perhaps homesick for the familiar creatures of England, a British settler released twenty-four imported rabbits near Melbourne in 1859. Unfortunately, there were not enough natural predators in Australia to keep in check a species that is extraordinarily prolific. Eagles and the wild dogs called dingoes might have helped, but their own numbers had been greatly reduced by ranchers, who considered them a threat to sheep herds. Within sixty years, rabbits had spread across the entire southern half of the continent, devouring native grasses and leaving desolation and dust in their wake. The rabbits not only dispossessed many indigenous animals as they spread, they also destroyed millions of acres of sheep pasturage. At Coongie Lakes, Julien Reid had shown us land still being denuded by descendants of those first rabbits. Ever expanding, the rabbits strip away vegetative cover by overgrazing and hasten erosion as they dig burrows in the ground. Several commercial rabbit shooters had been hired to kill rabbits in the Coongie area, but, as elsewhere in the country, their efforts seemed to make little dent in the rabbit population.

The spread of rabbits fueled a related increase in the number of imported foxes in Australia. Introduced by settlers who longed for the traditional fox hunts of England, the foxes found a predatory windfall in the swarms of rabbits, and followed them across the continent, endangering as they spread other native prey, such as possums, ground-nesting birds, and tortoises.

Besides erecting thousands of miles of fencing to corral rabbits—which proved a generally useless endeavor—Europeans released domestic cats as a means of controlling them. There is no evidence the cats had much effect on the rabbits, but instead multiplied along with their prey and spread as well throughout the continent as feral hunters, further depleting and displacing indigenous animals.

While the rabbit and fox invasions stemmed from attempts to re-create the English countryside, seemingly harmless agricultural schemes also caused unexpected results. Farmers trying to develop a sugar cane industry along the eastern and northeastern coast were hampered by a beetle, whose larvae attack cane. To remedy the problem, they imported from Hawaii a toad used for pest control. As a result, one of Australia's most problematic and ubiquitous alien invaders is the six-inch-long cane toad. Once again, an imported creature failed to accomplish its intended task, became a pest itself, and multiplied prolifically. Today, cane toads continue to expand northward and westward across the continent, posing a unique problem because they carry a potent poison in their skins and in parotid glands on the sides of their heads. Predatory animals that eat the toads usually die, as do household pets.

Imported plants have also turned into ravagers of the native land. A cactus called the prickly pear—planted as an ornamental hedge and as food for a beetle that is harvested for its natural dye—grew uncontrollably until it had occupied more than seventy-six million acres of the east and southeast. The planting of wheat in vast areas of the country eliminated habitat for some bird species, while fueling the disruptive growth of others. Moreover, the fields of wheat provided a new food for locusts, which had regularly traveled down inland eastern Australia for millions of years. By supporting

Overleaf:
The River Murray, Australia's largest and most important waterway, heads westward from its Snowy Mountains source through green foothills before descending to the flat southeastern interior of the country. (Called the River Murray in south Australia, it is the Murray River in Victoria and New South Wales.)

increased locust populations, wheat and other grain crops turned once-limited outbreaks into plagues that have raged across parts of the country every fifteen to twenty years.

The conquest of Australia probably seemed like such a simple proposition to early European settlers, who assumed they could turn an ugly land into something resembling the greener country they had come from, who surmised that agricultural techniques so successful in Europe could be transferred to this new land, and who had been educated to believe that with hard work and cleverness they could make even a desert productive. In some places, they prevailed, but even in areas now considered showplaces of Australian know-how and ingenuity, they often planted the seeds of ecological problems that now threaten to undermine progress.

As we traveled about the country, we were told by scientists and wildlife managers that perhaps no part of Australia better illustrates this dilemma than the Murray Basin. With its long tributary, the Darling River, the Murray drains one-seventh of Australia. It is to the southern continent roughly what the Mississippi is to America. With the coming of Europeans, the Murray was looked upon as a key to creating agricultural fields to support national expansion and prosperity. The success of such attempts is reflected today in the fact that half of Australia's food and fiber is linked to River Murray irrigation. But, we were told, there were impending ecological disasters looming along the Murray.

Accordingly, I dispatched Ian Chapman and Philippe Morice on a reconnaissance mission to determine whether our expedition should include a visit to the River Murray. After tracing the waterway from its origins in the Great Dividing Range, which rises about a hundred miles inland from the southeastern coast, and making several downriver stops, the two scouts returned to recommend enthusiastically that we venture down the Murray.

The Murray-Darling combined river system is the fourth longest in the world. Our plan was not to cover the entire length of the river from source to sea, for that was a journey of more than 1,500 miles and would not fit our schedule. We elected to fly or drive to strategic points along the river and to explore its vast midsection aboard a chartered houseboat. The prospects for a comfortable journey set well with the outback land team—Morice, Chapman, Wilcox, Jackson, Westgate, and Anne-Marie—all of whom were weary of bedrolls and sponge baths. On a morning in mid-October, at the river port of Mildura, they eagerly stowed their gear aboard a boxy houseboat that seemed something like a floating motel but was far homier than the all-terrain vehicles to which they had become accustomed. As the rental brochure promised, there was a hot shower, kitchen, refrigerator, beds, and

bedding. Joining the team at their departure, I could sense an easy ambiance aboard the houseboat, born of the return from the harsh Outback to a more familiar world. Around the breakfast table, laughter mingled with the smell of bacon and fresh croissants. We were, after all, ineluctably linked by heritage and education to the amenities of Western culture. We were, like the immigrants who had been coming here for 200 years, products of the behavioral patterns and mentality of Europe.

Though the Murray has been profoundly altered by newcomers, it is still possible to catch glimpses of wildlife along its more serene stretches. From the decks of the houseboat, we could see an occasional kangaroo bound away at our approach. We drifted past flocks of pelicans, gazed at galahs and cockatoos in the red gum trees that line the banks of the river. And we saw as well the newer lords of the land, rabbits and sheep grazing in grasslands adjacent to the Murray.

Near Mildura, we came upon a keepsake of river history—an old paddle steamer originally built as a workboat to haul supplies and to serve crews clearing fallen trees or building bridges and weirs across the Murray. Today, the *Melbourne* is operated as a tourist attraction, lazily carrying

Now a tourist attraction, the paddlesteamer Melbourne *was originally built as a River Murray workboat. Similar paddlesteamers turned the river into a highway through the bush, carrying European immigrants on a mission to settle and farm the empty interior.*

vacationers on two-hour cruises twice each day. Captain Alby Pointon, who restored the old vessel and pilots her, invited us aboard for a tour. He waved proudly at the boat's shiny original engine and boiler, still fired with wood. On the bridge, standing at his huge red steering wheel, he regaled us with stories of life along the Murray when squatters grazed their sheep and cattle along the banks and paddle steamers like the *Melbourne* supplied farmers with everything from plows and roofing iron to window glass and pianos, in turn carrying wool and other produce back to markets.

Early settlers had first used the river as a water highway into the southeastern interior of the continent, and as a lifeline of support in barren territory. The first steam-powered boats appeared on the Murray in 1853 and, until they were gradually replaced by railroads, served as agents of the European campaign to open up and exploit the most arable inland region of the continent.

But as villages and farmfields grew along the Murray, settlers realized that the river upon which they now depended for irrigation and transport was dangerously unreliable. In its natural state, the river mirrored the cyclical drought-and-flood regime of the land. Winter and spring waters could be abundant, but during the summer and fall, and also during severe droughts, the Murray was often reduced in places to a chain of saline waterholes. Aboriginal peoples had long adapted to the natural fluctuations of the river, but if European settlers were going to develop the Murray Basin intensively, they would have to make the river more reliable. A succession of drought years at the turn of the century drove them to seek ways to domesticate the untamed River Murray.

With supreme confidence, farmers turned to proven Western technology and engineering. A grand scheme of dams, locks, weirs, and a hundred reservoir lakes were imposed upon the Murray during the first half of this century, transforming it from a wild waterway into something entirely different—an immense irrigation system elaborately regulated to supply crops and people with a dependable water source in a rain-starved land. From a commercial point of view, the harnessing of the Murray was enormously successful. Today, nearly two million acres are irrigated by Murray water. Citrus orchards and vegetable fields form wide green belts along the river. Rice and other grains blanket land that was once barren. Dairy and beef cattle graze on Murray-irrigated pasture. Australians look upon the Murray Valley as their vital food basket and export generator, supplier not only of the staples of human nourishment but the luxuries as well, from wine and almonds to avocados, olives, and oranges.

But regulation of the river has produced detrimental side effects as well, some of them not only unintended but unimagined. By inserting dams and weirs into the river, engineers· effectively blocked the migration of many river fish to their breeding grounds, and once-common species such as the Murray cod, silver perch, and golden perch have diminished in number as a result.

Joining Dr. Michael Geddes, a biologist from the University of Adelaide, we saw at close range another native of the river which has nearly disappeared in the aftermath of the schemes to control river water for human use. When Europeans first waded into the Murray they discovered an abundance of large crayfish, also called Murray lobsters, which proved to be both easy to harvest and delicious. Second only to a Tasmanian crayfish as the world's largest, the Murray cray can reach a length of twelve inches and a weight of seven pounds. Though the cray supported a popular fishery, there is no evidence that overfishing caused a mysterious near-disappearance of Murray crays in the 1940s and 50s. Today, the crayfish is locally extinct downriver of Mildura and rare upriver and in tributaries of the Murray.

As Dr. Geddes explained, scientists today theorize that a combination of effects caused by dams and weirs made it difficult for the creatures to survive. Siltation rates increased with the introduction of weirs, with the result that deep depressions in the river bottom—a prime habitat of crayfish—were steadily filled. Also, both the oxygen level and the temperature of river water were altered in some places by the creation of static reservoirs. A drop in the oxygen level may have contributed to the decline in cray populations, and a drop in the water temperature may have hampered spawning. Finally, pesticides sprayed in the Murray Valley to fight locust plagues in the early 1950s may have washed into the river and killed countless crayfish.

The abundance of irrigation water has backfired in parts of the Murray Valley. In flooded fields, water tables rise, flushing upward deep layers of salts deposited by ancient seas. When saturated with salts, agricultural lands become useless. Farmers and scientists today struggle to correct an unanticipated problem that threatens the nation's "food basket."

Dr. Geddes invited us to accompany him in a small motorboat, laden with instruments and cages. In a project funded by the University of Adelaide, the Warrnambool Institute, and the River Murray Commission, Geddes is seeking to learn precisely what caused the decline of the crayfish and if conditions in the River Murray today will permit a reintroduction of the creatures to their native habitat. Juveniles are allowed to mature in tanks and pools, then caged individually or as mating pairs and lowered in cages to the river bottom, where their condition is carefully monitored. Extensive evaluation of water quality at a variety of test sites will enable Geddes to gauge growth and breeding success according to specific water conditions. If Geddes's caged crays survive, a restocking program will begin. If the test animals die, Geddes hopes he can trace the cause of the problem and identify remedies. If the source of the decline proves to be integral to the dam and weir system, however, the crays may be doomed. As suggested in literature from the River Murray Commission—the agency in charge of regulation—Murray Valley communities long ago concluded that the benefits of development and prosperity outweighed potential damage to parts of their natural environment.

Exploring the river near Paringa by Zodiac one morning, Clay Wilcox came upon a couple who seemed to regret the secondary importance assigned to the health of river life. John and Cecile Aston were casting fishing nets into calm, dawn-lit pools of the Murray, as they have nearly every morning for forty years. Working from a small skiff, they have managed to make a living from the fish hauled out daily, which are transported to market in camping coolers that fill the bed of their pickup.

Wilcox was charmed by the lively, colloquial wit of the Astons, who seemed to welcome his company and his curiosity about the river that had long flowed through their lives. They were eager also to voice their complaints about river management, which, they contended, had made commercial fishing an increasingly difficult enterprise.

"We've locked the river with irrigation from end to end," John said, "and this, in turn, has upset the native fish population immensely. We've caused it to go down; it's not the fish who did it. We've blocked the rivers, and we've stopped the river from flushing as it did in past years. It's as simple as that."

As the Astons hauled the skiff ashore and sorted their catch, they introduced Wilcox to the River Murray equivalent of the rabbit—the European carp. Grimacing, Cecile held up a thirty-inch, humpbacked fish with a small mouth bearing barbels at each corner. She pointed to the dorsal fin. "We don't like these blokes," she said, "because they cut our nets to pieces. The dorsal fin is like a very sharp rasp, and he gets it tangled up in our nets and just goes around and around until he breaks the cords. And we've got to

mend nets every day. They also eat the babies of a fish we call the red fin, quite a nice fish to eat. They're a menace."

There are accounts of the presence of European carp in Australia as early as 1872, perhaps imported to please the palates of settlers accustomed to carp meals back home. Like rabbits, European carp are wildly fertile. John Aston slit open the belly of a mature female to show Wilcox the gray egg mass. On average, the females lay half a million eggs at a time, and they do so several times a year. By comparison, many native fish spawn only once annually. "There's a jolly lot that survive," said John, "a jolly lot. They're just a blinking nuisance."

Besides supplanting some native species, the carp also change the river, said the Astons, by rooting about the bottom for food. The constantly muddied waters make it more difficult for other fish species to survive. Suspended sediments block sunlight from the bottom, impeding the growth of aquatic plants upon which some other species depend. Though the European carp is recognized by fishermen and scientists alike as a harmful scourge, it remains as uncontrollable in the river as the rabbit is on the land.

Perhaps the greatest menace to the Murray Valley arises not only from modifications to the present-day river but from remains of the ancient ocean. We were told by people along the river that salts deposited millions of years ago, when the area was beneath the sea, are returning to haunt and to threaten vast areas now planted with food crops. Following their initial scouting trip along the Murray, Morice and Chapman had briefed us on this strange story, but we did not realize the scope of the potential catastrophe until we interviewed Murray scientists and farmers and saw the problem in handfuls of dead soil.

Once again, settlers could envision nothing harmful in clearing away trees with no commercial value—commonly the small variety of eucalyptus called mallee in Australia—and soaking the resulting croplands with Murray water in order to turn the desert green. But the countless tons of water flooding farmlands over decades has raised water-table levels in some areas, flushing deep layers of salts upward to the surface or very near it. The irrigation water evaporates, but the salts accumulate. The problem is twofold, caused not only by the huge volume of water pumped onto fields that once received only minimal rainfall but also by the substitution of shallow-rooted plants and grasses for the native, deep-rooted vegetation, which took in more groundwater and kept water tables low.

When saturated with salt crystals, the land is useless for existing agriculture. Farmers look upon the invisible flood of salt rising beneath their land as a kind of monster. They refer to it as the "White Death" and dread its appearance on their land, which means the end of their livelihood and a financial debacle. Already, Australian authorities estimate that more than 865,000 acres of Australian farmland have been killed by salinity, and that two and a half million acres may be dead by the year 2000. Mal Brown, a Salinity Education Officer for the Department of Agriculture, led us to a small pond on the land of a fruit grower. Using a salinity meter, he showed us that the water, supposed to be fresh, was fifty percent saltier than seawater.

The salinity problem also ricochets back to the Murray itself. Salt-tainted rain runoff and underground seepage drain into the river, increasing the salinity of the Murray as it flows downstream. Since the river is the principal source of drinking water not only for river towns but for the large industrial centers near its delta, including Adelaide with a population in excess of a million people, the problem has far-reaching implications for the future. Already, a survey of public water supplies in Western Australia has revealed that a third are saltier than the highest desirable level determined by the World Health Organization.

Along a salt-damaged stretch of the riverbank, we came upon agronomist Tim Cummins, who has made resolving the salinity problem the focus of his professional life. He told us that the water beneath our houseboat was roughly ten times saltier than it should be. Moreover, the rise of salinity was not limited to Australia, he said. He quoted a United Nations Food and Agriculture Organization study which estimated that several hundred thousand hectares (a hectare is about two and a half acres) of irrigated land worldwide are abandoned annually as a result of salinization. The FAO estimates that fifty percent of the world's irrigated land now suffers from salinization—more than a hundred million acres.

Australian scientists and growers are now engaged in a desperate race to halt salt encroachment before it destroys more of the nation's most productive agricultural fields. Farmers test new irrigation systems designed to save water, and experiment with plants that can tolerate salt. Ironically, perhaps the most promising remedy is the replanting of mallee and other native, deep-rooted trees to help suck up excess irrigation water before it can reach the water table. In other words, the solution may lie in partially re-creating the ancient environment that generations of settlers have tried to erase.

With Morice, Westgate, and Anne-Marie, I flew to Albury, a small upriver town not far from the flanks of the Snowy Mountains, where the Murray tumbles westward through forested slopes toward the interior flatlands. There I spoke at length with Dr. David Mitchell, Director of the Murray-Darling Freshwater Research Centre, and Dr. Terry Hillman, Officer in Charge. Mitchell, Hillman, and their colleagues conduct laboratory work to analyze the impact on the river system of every important modern activity, from agricultural exploitation to off-road vehicles and boating. Their goal is not only to identify important problems, but also to foresee and help determine Australia's fresh-water future.

For Mitchell and Hillman, the threats to the Murray extend beyond issues of water quality to the aesthetic nature of the waterway and its role as a national symbol. After taking us on a tour of the research center, they led me to a vista overlooking the Murray. Far upriver it was a bright, fast mountain stream, turned here to a sluggish channel, soon to widen downriver into the brown, thoroughly regulated irrigator of fields. Crossing the flat desert, it once meandered like a lazy snake. Sudden floods quickly washed over the curves to form a vast floodplain. The dams and weirs changed all that.

"Parts of this Murray River system are quintessentially Australian," Mitchell told me. "You won't find anything else like it anywhere in the world. And it's very precious to Australians. It's very evocative of the country in which they live, and they'd like it to remain. It's a great natural resource."

Hillman said that as a scientist, he worried that programs to transfigure the river for human purposes might be jeopardizing its very existence. "If we don't have a viable floodplain ecosystem, maybe we won't have a river in the long term," he said. "We may be trying to go too far in managing the river. I guess scientists like me are saying: that river is a living system, not just a water supply. Maybe we've got to understand enough about it so that we can maintain it as a living system, because otherwise the water supply will collapse as well."

Overleaf:
Looming like stone pilings,
rock formations off the
Tasmanian coast serve as a
warning to Alcyone's *team of*
a rugged shoreline notorious
among mariners. Caught in
storms racing up from
Antarctica, the ships of
traders and explorers
foundered against these rocky
shores and now litter the
undersea flanks of Tasmania.

Months earlier, while diving along the coast of Tasmania from *Alcyone,* we had met several people who told us that the struggle to preserve a healthy environment for future generations of Australians, the war between vested interests and conservationists for the soul of the country, was being waged most fiercely not on the mainland of Australia but on the island of Tasmania. Now curious to learn more about the challenges facing the country, we returned to Tasmania in *Alcyone.*

Tasmania abounds in a lush, majestic beauty that is rare on the great dry continent little more than a hundred miles to the north. Abundant rainfall sweeps across the island, producing forested mountains washed by swift, year-round streams. The interior reaches are characterized by a unique variety of dense woodland, which goes by the name rain forest yet is far different from the tropical rain forests we had explored in the Amazon and Papua New Guinea. Tasmania's temperate rain forests thrive in cold weather, even survive under an occasional blanketing of winter snow. There are no palm trees here, nor climbing liana vines, but trees such as myrtle, beech, sassafras, leatherwood, and several kinds of pine. When the British settled in Tasmania in 1803, seventy-two percent of the island was covered in dense woods. Today, rain forests endure on about forty percent of Tasmania's land area.

We wanted to trek into this unusual, temperate jungle, so we steered *Alcyone* through Macquarie Harbour on the west coast, then up the Gordon River, a still-wild waterway that takes a tortuous course as it weaves seaward among the flanks of the Elliot Range. Beneath a steady drizzle, we stood on the deck of *Alcyone* in spellbound silence as we entered what seemed to be a cool, shady, and wet Eden. Fortunately, we were accompanied by Bob Ingles, regional manager of the Tasmanian Forestry Commission, who supplied names for the trees and plants that covered the banks and hillsides in a tangled profusion of green hues. Dense mosses, lichens, and fungi covered the bark of myrtles and pines, and every inch of space between the trees seemed occupied by some variety of fern or low shrub, all of this underlain by rich dark soil and black peat—and glistening with misty rain.

Along the banks, tiny waterfalls cascaded through the moss and into the river, which was brackish as a result of tannin runoff from button grass. Cormorants sat at the edge of the green tableau, warily watching our passage, while sea eagles circled in the air above.

We left *Alcyone* by Zodiac for a closer inspection. As we stepped on spongy soil, looked about at the jumble of ferns and trees and exposed roots, and smelled the earthy fragrance of the rain forest, Arrington broke the silence by pronouncing the scene "Tolkien-like." The almost impenetrable riverine woods were at times so dense beneath our feet that we

actually traversed it six feet above the ground. Climbing from limb to limb, Rosset slipped and crashed to the forest floor. We stopped while he cursed and laughed, then pulled himself up from the shadows covered in mud like a rugby player. Quickly, the patter of our voices died away, and the heavy silence flooded over us again.

As we approached a towering tree, Bob Ingles held up his hand, as if we had happened upon something sacred. The tree, he explained, was a Huon pine, a species unique to Tasmania.

"You are standing in the presence of a Methuselah," said Bob. "Huon pines grow only about five inches per century, and some reach several hundred feet. There have been many large Huon pines that were more than 2,000 years old, making them probably Australia's oldest trees. And the lineage is ancient. Pollen records of the Huon pine family date back at least 135 million years."

We asked about the age of the tree before us. "Some estimate that it could be up to 5,000 years old," he said.

"Are you saying it could be the oldest living thing on earth?" I asked.

"Could be," Bob said.

A logging truck passes through the Tasmanian capital of Hobart. Forestry has been a major industry in the island state since the arrival of Europeans in 1803. At the time, nearly three quarters of the island was covered in temperate rainforests. Today, about forty percent of Tasmania is wooded.

(The tree was toppled by the fall of another giant pine about a year after our visit.)

There was more than historical value to the tree, he told us. Calculating silently for a few seconds, he estimated that if the entire tree were felled, and sold by a sawmiller, it would probably bring between $40,000 and $60,000.

"Then why is it still standing here?" asked Rosset.

"The local sawmiller decided that this particular tree is so large and so unique that it should stay here."

But the decision of the local sawmiller, he told us, was unusual in the sweep of Tasmanian history. The Huon pine spawned one of Tasmania's first industries, and most of the trees standing here when Europeans arrived are long gone.

The Huon pine offers several characteristics that have made it extraordinarily valuable. Furniture makers found that its wood was soft, closely grained, extremely durable and fragrant. As the supply of timber declined, the price escalated. A new Huon pine cabinet—fashioned from the scattered remains of trees logged nearly a century ago—can carry a showroom price of $12,000 today.

But perhaps the most notable distinction of Huon pine is its ranking as one of the finest shipbuilding woods in the world. Oil can account for up to seven percent of the wood's weight, making it almost completely rot-resistant. Timber debris—called heads and butts—found lying in areas logged eighty years ago is still of sufficient quality to be used in fine woodworking and boat building.

For arriving immigrants, Huon pine provided a kind of green gold. Boatyards became major elements of the developing Tasmanian economy, and the most accessible stands of a tree that took centuries to mature were quickly felled. What was not cut down was drowned ultimately, as Tasmania undertook a massive program of hydroelectric dam building. Bob Ingles told us that political schemes to create jobs through large construction projects doomed vast areas of the remaining rain forest. The dams eventually drew the ire of conservationists, who argued that Tasmania already had a surplus of hydroelectric energy. When the state Hydro-Electric Commission proposed in 1979 to dam the Franklin and lower Gordon Rivers, massive protests erupted. A three-year controversy—which included a citizen blockade of barges carrying construction equipment up the Gordon and the eventual arrest of more than a thousand protesters—ended in a constitutional showdown and the defeat of the dam project. Today, environmentalists consider their victory a watershed event in national history, and the first proof of an emerging Australian environmental ethic.

Sheep file across the slopes of a Tasmanian sheep ranch. Early immigrants to Australia from Europe, ignorant of the fragility of the continent's arid environment, assumed that the land would support huge sheep ranches. For the most part, it did, but fragile soils and grasses—upon which no hoof had ever stepped—were trampled into wastelands in parts of the country. Nevertheless, sheep remain the quintessential and prolific symbol of Australia's rural economy. Even today, there are ten times more sheep than people in the country.

From a cool, forested dreamland, we traveled to a landscape as barren and lifeless as the surface of the moon. In hill country just north of the Gordon River, a mining operation has extracted a million tons of gold, silver, and copper during the past century. When opened in 1883, the Mt. Lyell mine near Queenstown was nestled into rain forests similar to those flanking the Gordon River. Since then, logging, fire, and sulfurous fumes from copper smelting have extinguished every living thing across fifteen square miles. Scattered among the rocky, denuded slopes we spotted a few splintered and dead tree trunks, which looked to me like hoary fingers pointing crookedly at the sky.

Historically, mining followed agriculture as a second great lure drawing immigrants to the southern continent. Rich copper deposits were first discovered in South Australia in the 1840s; iron ore was first mined in 1848, and when gold was discovered near Bathurst in 1851, the rush to find riches in Australia was on. Between 1861 and 1909, each colony or state of the continent was at one time the world's leading producer of gold, silver, lead, copper, tin, or coal.

We were told that the Mt. Lyell mine is scheduled to close soon, threatening a once-booming local economy. Ironically, the wasteland left behind now supports people in Queenstown by drawing, of all things, tourism. So blighted is the land, so scoured of life, that some 40,000 tourists come each year to gaze at the remains.

Chapman asked Joyce Bushby, who operates a popular mine tour, what attracts so many visitors. "I always describe Queenstown as 'God's Country,'" she said. "It's so different, so unique. It's like a lunar landscape."

Scientists estimate that, even under ideal conditions, it could take 500 years for something resembling the original rainforest to return. Some hillsides, abandoned by the mine decades ago, have begun to sprout a thin covering of grass and saltbush, a development that worries the local tourist industry. There are campaigns afoot today to save the mine from regrowth. Joyce Bushby hopes that at least some of the ravaged land can be kept as it is—dead. "We'd like to preserve a small portion so that people can see it," she said, "as it is one of our biggest tourist attractions. It's there, it's happened, we can't do anything about it."

Bushby and others propose that new vegetation be removed as it appears. Yet they reject plans to spray herbicides. The century of mine operation taught the people of Queenstown something about pollution. In addition to the sulfur-tainted air, decades of eroded silt and cast off mine debris have suffocated the once-pristine Queen River. Accordingly, tour operators recommend that returning vegetation be cleansed from the hillsides by hand.

The devastation caused by the Mt. Lyell mine is an exception. Most of Australia's mining operations have produced less dramatic impacts on the living environment around them. But the spread of mines greatly increased the demand for lumber. Wood was needed for struts and supports in the mines themselves, as fuel for the steam engines used in mining, and to build housing for the influx of new miners. Timber harvesting became such a major Australian industry in Tasmania and along the coastal belt of forests surrounding much of the continent that two thirds of the original forests soon disappeared.

The loss of woodlands escalated with the advent of modern industrial forestry methods, such as clear cutting, in which all of the trees in an area are felled using heavy machinery. Opponents today argue that the method not only extinguishes old-growth forests but compacts the soil and causes erosion, leaving the ground unfit for reseeding. Forestry companies replace the cut forest with plantations of fast-growing trees, such as eucalyptus and pine, which usually are turned to wood chips or pulp for various paper industries.

Wastes dumped into the sea from a pulp mill at Burnie, Tasmania, produce a toxic, foam-covered surf. Residents who swim in the sea nearby emerge with rashes. Protests against proposals to build another mill in the area focused attention on environmental abuses throughout Tasmania, and helped spawn a citizen movement that has reverberated not only throughout the island but across the continent itself.

As in other parts of the world, foresters and forest protectors argue over the wisdom of substituting a monoculture of a single species for the mixed species of native forests. Commercial exploiters believe that small patches of native forest will suffice to support indigenous animal life; environmentalists fear that dwindling old-growth woodlands will mean the irrevocable end of certain species, as well as the deterioration of natural beauty and diversity.

Returning to *Alcyone*, we sailed to the town of Burnie along the northern coast of Tasmania, where a related controversy was raging. Some sixty percent of Tasmania's timber is exported for wood chipping. Of what remains, the greatest profits derive from turning logs into bleached pulp, which is used to make paper and paper products, and commands a high price in Japan as well as in Australia itself. Tasmanian involvement in the pulping business began when a pulp mill was opened at Burnie in 1938. The Burnie mill was of interest to us principally because it is the precursor to a proposed one-billion dollar pulp mill that would be built nearby at Wesley Vale, and would be, according to local opponents, the largest pulp mill in the world.

When we arrived in Burnie, we spoke with Christine Milne, a local schoolteacher who had reluctantly assumed leadership of the citizens' group opposed to the mill. She told Chapman that the mill, employing a sulfur-chlorine process, would emit a foul odor, and that it would also discharge organochlorine compounds, including dioxin, into the air and the nearby ocean.

"And we believe," she said, "that this is totally inappropriate for the future direction we want Tasmania to take. People feel they've worked very hard to develop the local land for farming. They've cared for it, nurtured it, and they had hoped to hand it on to their children and to future generations. And they see now what's happening as nothing short of vandalism. That in Tasmania, we've lost control to multinationals. That the government seems so intent on accommodating these companies and virtually giving away our resources that they've forgotten who they are supposed to be representing. We've got this wonderful alternative where we have small labor-intensive industries that are Tasmanian-owned, environmentally friendly, ecologically sustainable. People say, you can't beat back such powerful people, but our power will stop these mills."

To understand the effect of such operations on the environment, our team arranged for a visit to the existing Burnie pulp mill. We had been forewarned by mill critics to expect smoke belching from the mill smokestack. There was none. A spokesman for the mill told us that no visible smoke was emitted, that the Burnie mill had installed a pollution-free stack.

A day later, we learned from reliable sources that the mill had been shut down during our visit, presumably to offer our cameras a positive appearance. One local man told us the mill had been shut down only once before— ten years ago during a visit by Queen Elizabeth. We found no way to verify the story, but we decided to make an unannounced visit several days later. This time, dense white smoke rose from the smokestack and drifted like a fog across the town of Burnie. Along a beach in front of the mill, the surf was blanketed by a foul white foam several feet thick, visible evidence of the pollution piped from the mill into the ocean. The mine spokesman said such

Cousteau diver Capkin Van Alphen holds a wombat, a marsupial cousin of the koala that is found only in Australia. Unlike koalas, wombats shun trees and live a rodent-like existence, remaining in underground burrows during the day and emerging at night to graze.

an occurrence was rare, the result of uncommon northeast winds preventing the waste from washing out to sea.

Chapman found Anna Wind, a young woman from Burnie, walking along the beach with her child. The foam was a common sight here, she told him, and since there were no warning signs posted, children from the area swam in it regularly. She wouldn't allow her children to go in the ocean, however, since the water seemed to cause strange rashes.

When we departed Burnie, Christine Milne was running for the state parliament on a "no-mill, pro-environment" platform. The future of Tasmania's forests and of the pulp mill industry had become issues on which the entire election would turn. Months later, we learned that Milne had been elected, to the surprise of her opposition, and the Wesley Vale mill had been defeated. A special United Nations citation commended Christine Milne for her courageous efforts on behalf not only of the environment but the quality of life of future generations in Tasmania.

Ironically, the movement to preserve Australia's environmental legacy seemed to be strongest in a part of the nation that had been notorious earlier for its plundering of native forests and its insensitivity toward Aboriginal peoples. Tasmania's European settlers not only threatened the survival of such invaluable tree species as the Huon pine, they also eradicated the Tasmanian tiger—a marsupial wolf with stripes across its back, more correctly called a thylacine, which was perceived as a threat to sheep herds. The Tasmanian government acted to protect thylacines in 1936, but it was too late. The last known thylacine died in a Hobart zoo about the same time. Some still hold out hope that a living thylacine will walk out of the woods some day, and there are reports nearly every year of a sighting, but no living

Shrieking howls and a ferocious appearance earned Tasmanian devils their formidable name and reputation, but these carrion eaters can easily be killed by a dog if forced to fight. Once they roamed much of the continent, but competition from, and perhaps predation by dingoes, has eliminated the devils from all but Tasmania.

153

or dead specimens have been found in the wild and it is likely that the creature is extinct.

Tasmania's original inhabitants, about 5,000 Aboriginals, suffered the same fate as the thylacine. British settlers regarded the natives as subhuman beings and hunted them down like wild game. Within thirty years, the Aboriginal population had been reduced to a few hundred people, and when one of the last full-blooded Tasmanian natives died—a woman named Truganini—her skeleton went on display, as if it represented, like dinosaur bones, an alien form of life.

That the descendants of the settlers who exterminated life so callously should be among the leaders of the movement to preserve Australia's natural world seemed to us a societal turnabout of great import and great promise.

The end of our expedition approached.

We had glided through the Great Barrier Reef, wandered the Outback, swum with snakes and dragons and mermaids, touched the dry bones of primeval seas, trekked the forests of Tasmania, tagged great white sharks, eaten grubs and the nectar of honey ants, endured the daily agony of flies as relentless and rude as any in the world, captured two platypuses, contemplated the magic of the dreaming, and connected with a culture far more ancient than our own.

Yet there remained a sublime and precious world still to be encountered, a corner of the continent as large as Israel and as exotic as the Amazon, a wild considered one of the purest and least-changed places on earth. So valuable is this region on a global scale that the United Nations in 1981 declared it a World Heritage Property, an honor it shares with the Grand Canyon, the Pyramids, and the Cathedral at Chartres, among other sites. It was the first area of Australia deemed worthy of inclusion on the World Heritage list.

It is called Kakadu—a 7,650-square-mile plot of land in the north that is the largest and biologically richest national park in Australia. Within its boundaries lie all of the major habitat types of the continent's tropical northern reaches, the so-called Top End. But Kakadu seems in its seasonal shifts through monsoonal inundation and searing aridity, in its bizarre mingling of tropical forests and desert grasses, to capture the immoderate, enigmatic character of the entire continent.

A shelflike sandstone escarpment scored with deep gorges looms above rocky outcrops, monsoon and eucalyptus forests, grassy savanna and floodplains, tidal rivers and flats, mangrove forests, and coastal swamps. As if fashioned by nature as a living museum, Kakadu contains a third of all Australia's bird species and a quarter of the country's freshwater fish

Opposite:
Spectacular Jim Jim Falls in Kakadu National Park drops a sheer 650 feet into a seemingly bottomless, boulder-strewn pool. Unique natural and cultural features of Kakadu—whose name derives from the local Gagadju Aboriginal people— led the United Nations to declare it Australia's first World Heritage Property in 1981.

A royal spoonbill heads toward its marshy feeding grounds in Kakadu. Spoonbills briskly sweep their distinctive bills from side to side in shallow water, locating small aquatic prey by touch with the sensitive tips of their bills. About a third of all Australia's bird species are found in Kakadu, and it serves as a vital refuge for waterbirds like the spoonbill.

species, including the barramundi, which can weigh a hundred pounds. Kangaroos, wallabies, and dingoes roam parts of Kakadu, as do echidnas, marsupial mice, ghost bats, rock possums. Kakadu's incredible diversity is reflected in a curious fact: there are a hundred species of ants per acre in the park. Another fact illustrates the region's remoteness from human impact: since records have been kept, Kakadu has not lost a single species of plant or animal.

We were, of course, intent upon taking a close look at such a place, but we were interested in Kakadu for a more profound reason. Kakadu seemed to us a symbol of the challenges facing Australia in the future. Our research suggested that multiple forces were at work in Kakadu: the awakening national concern for environmental preservation, which had led to the declaration of the region as a park in 1979; the legacy of past mistakes, such as introduced species; and pressures to develop and exploit resources within the park, despite its protected status. Moreover, the present-day park had once supported an Aboriginal people—the Gagudju, whose name was corrupted to Kakadu by an early explorer. What was their current situation, and what lay ahead for the Aboriginals of Kakadu? Perhaps if we understood the future of this obscure and remote realm of Australia, we could envision the future environmental trend of the entire continent.

Six months earlier I had dispatched Dick Murphy on a reconnaissance trip to Kakadu. The Cousteau biologist often serves as our advance scout, collecting data, questioning local contacts, observing natural phenomena, identifying worthy subjects for our camera teams. Murphy has a doctorate in marine biology but he also has the mind-set of a mountain trapper,

The rich amphibian dwellers of Kakadu, like this tiny frog, create a nocturnal symphony during the wet season, as each species makes vocal music to attract mates.

preferring the independence and simplicity of solo trips. He will set off alone for any backwater or jungle tributary in the world carrying little more than his mask, snorkel, fins, camera, and cheap notebooks. A headband-mounted flashlight enables him to read and write in a tent far into the night, and a few tins of sardines suffice for his nourishment.

Murphy arrived in Kakadu at the beginning of the rainy season, or the Wet as it is known locally, and immediately became fascinated with the radical fluctuations of the park's seasons. Though the Aboriginals tradition-ally divide the year into at least six seasons, Westerners generally recognize only two, both of which represent extremes. The Wet is characterized by immense floods. The Dry brings severe drought and fires.

"Wildly simplified," Murphy told me later, "you have this beautiful tropical ecosystem that becomes wet and lush with the arrival of the monsoons. Life blooms everywhere across the flat floodplains. Gradually things dry out. The water recedes. Along come hot southeast winds to further parch the landscape. Fires erupt, set by lightning or Aboriginals, and the flames seem to ravage the dry land and kill the vegetation that

Expedition scientist Dr. Richard Murphy provides perspective on the immensity of a Kakadu termite nest. These massive mud structures can reach over twenty feet high and contain a sealed city for millions of termites.

seemed so luxuriant only months before. Then, suddenly, it starts all over again as the rains arrive to reirrigate and reinitiate life."

During Murphy's travels about Kakadu, he watched in amazement as hundreds of thousands of magpie geese descended on the park's waters. Once widely dispersed throughout the wetter regions of Australia, magpie geese now largely depend upon Kakadu for their survival. Sixty to seventy percent of the total species is found in the park during part of each year. Lanky black-and-white birds, the geese command attention during their stay, raising a honking clamor that can be heard miles away, and aggressively muddying park waterways as they root about for bulbs of the spike rush.

"To the casual observer," Murphy said, "the geese must seem like a gang of destroyers, ravaging and digging the place up. But in fact their work is something like plowing and fertilizing fields that will turn into grassy prairies as the waters recede. Particulars of each season can seem in isolation like terrible perturbations—the damages left by geese, the floods, the fires, the drought. But when looked upon from a grand perspective, each is a form of nourishment and preparation for what follows, collectively supporting an equilibrium that has kept the region dynamic across the aeons. In the drastic extremes of Kakadu, one sees more clearly than most places the yin and yang of nature on earth. Here, life and death—which begets new life which begets new death ad infinitum—are beautifully, artistically, poetically dramatized."

Murphy recommended that we send a camera crew to Kakadu.

Six months later, at the beginning of the Dry, Jean-Paul Cornu and Marc Blessington arrived to begin documenting the park on film. Cornu has been one of our most dependable surface (as opposed to underwater) cinematographers over the years, and the tales of his intrepid pursuit of good shots regardless of the personal cost are legion. He has been bitten by a Mississippi alligator, once broke several ribs and contracted a severe case of malaria in the Amazon, and nearly died of ciguatera poisoning in Haiti. His intensity, in fact, gave me pause when I contemplated sending him to Kakadu. The most famous resident of the park, the creature he would undoubtedly try to film at close range and in great detail, is the crocodile. The popular film *Crocodile Dundee* was filmed in part at Kakadu, and scenes of the huge reptiles emerging from the water to attack humans were not without a basis in fact. Most common in tidal rivers and floodplain billabongs (water holes), crocodiles had killed at least two tourists inside the park since it opened and as many as twenty-eight, we were told, throughout Australia during the past two decades. Accordingly, tourists in

At wet season, a river meanders over rugged rock outcroppings on the Arnhem Land Plateau, which rises along the eastern edge of Kakadu.

158

Kakadu are strictly forbidden to swim. A park brochure suggests that visitors never leave their boats, even if stranded.

Cornu promptly set about filming crocodiles. His inquiries about the best locations in which to find the animals met with warnings. Park rangers told of the Australian woman who was attacked while canoeing through the park. They emphasized the unpredictability of crocodile encounters. Only three days before Cornu's arrival, he learned, a film crew from an American television network had met with near disaster when a huge crocodile charged their boat, capsizing it. Luckily, the team escaped harm, but they lost all of their equipment and every roll of film they had shot.

Cornu, of course, rented a boat. However, he did make the concession of

Calypso *cinematographer Michel Deloire, ignoring the creature's vaunted reputation for attacking humans, films a saltwater crocodile along the bottom of the Jardine River on Cape York.*

hiring a heavy, broad-beamed boat unlikely to be turned over by anything smaller than a submarine. His decision probably derived from the fact that the stability of the vessel would enhance the steadiness of his shots. Another factor may have been that Kakadu tour operator and boat lessor Gordon Scarrow, a generous soul who welcomed the notion of a Cousteau film about a place he loves, offered the larger boat for free.

Cornu and Blessington cruised northward from their hotel in the center of the park to an immense floodplain called Munmarlary along the South Alligator River—a historical misnomer, since there are crocodiles in Kakadu but no alligators. (Alligators have broader snouts than crocodiles and there are minor differences in jaw structure between the two.) The tidal

A crocodile near Townsville displays the sudden lunge and bite, usually preceded by long periods of motionless rest, that instills fear in fellow denizens of the tropical wetlands, and in the humans who pass through.

rivers and billabongs of Munmarlary abound not only in crocodiles but in the fish and waterbirds that serve as favorite crocodile prey. Returning often to the same area during their three-month initial visit to Kakadu, and on four subsequent trips, Cornu and Blessington compiled a fascinating film record of bird life in Kakadu. They captured the quick, spunky dives of fishing cormorants, the heavy plummet of diving pelicans and the catlike stalk of herons, egrets, and ibises—which is followed by moments when the long-legged birds freeze, then suddenly pluck an unsuspecting fish from the swampy shallows. And they shot dramatic scenes as well of the elegant jabiru, a black-and-white stork whose coloring and impressive air have prompted the nickname policeman bird. Time and again as they filmed, a jabiru, seemingly distracted by its pursuit of fish, would become the target of a crocodile, which moved ever closer without causing a ripple in the water. Expecting to document a crocodile kill, Cornu and Blessington instead watched the cagey jabirus saunter on pipe-stem legs just ahead of the onrushing crocodiles, alertly sidestepping and frustrating each attack.

Both freshwater and saltwater crocodiles live in Kakadu, but it is the "saltie" that poses the greater danger to humans. Sometimes reaching a

A sign of the distant past and the arriving future—a crocodile-shaped tourist hotel in Jabiru designed and operated by the Gagadju people. While maintaining their traditions and protecting cave art tens of thousands of years old, the Gagadju of Kakadu have also entered the twentieth century.

length of twenty-three feet or more and a weight in excess of a ton, saltwater crocodiles are formidable enough to attack and consume water buffalos. Analyses of their stomach contents have revealed as well the remains of dingoes, wallabies, turtles, snakes, bats, crabs, fish, birds, domestic cats and dogs, cattle, and other crocodiles.

During *Calypso's* mission along the Great Barrier Reef, a film team had managed a spectacular, and historic, confrontation with an Australian saltwater crocodile. Traveling up the Jardine River, which empties into the sea at the tip of the Cape York Peninsula, the team was forewarned that they were courting danger; local people told them a drunken man had been devoured by a saltwater crocodile three weeks earlier at the very spot where they hoped to dive.

While studying crocodile tracks along a sand bank, the team disturbed a resting crocodile, which darted into the river. Biologist Sarano, cameraman Deloire, and photographer Noirot followed, donning masks and snorkels, slipping into the river, but quickly losing sight of their subject in water with less than ten feet of visibility.

Sarano drifted about, mesmerized by other river life. He watched fish pass in silver flashes, found a python coiled in rocks, then turned to take hold of a rotting branch along the bottom. Fortunately, just as he was about to grab it, Sarano recognized the branch as the tail of the saltwater crocodile he sought. The creature appeared to be about ten feet long, perhaps about twelve years old. The crocodile was motionless, and Sarano, for obvious reasons, was equally still. Without losing sight of the reptile, the biologist slowly rose to the surface and beckoned for Deloire, but the approach of the cameraman spooked the crocodile, which shot away, leaving a cloud of sand in its wake.

From above, Ivan Giacoletto followed the crocodile's charge. It had stopped about 300 feet downstream. The divers drifted in pursuit and found the crocodile in a deep depression of the river bottom, as still as a log again. This time the creature "granted an audience," as Sarano put it, and the team hovered within arm's length of the alleged "man killer" for nearly an hour. At one point, emboldened by the seeming passivity of the crocodile, Sarano stroked its back as if it was a sleepy cocker spaniel. To his surprise, the armored scales presented a deceiving picture; the skin felt soft and smooth. Sarano slipped along the creature's side to study its tail, aware it could whip about at any moment with the force of a deadly weapon. But intuition told the biologist it would not.

In fact, the crocodile remained motionless. It stared at the diver through swiveling, gold-and-green eyes, but revealed no hint of annoyance, fear, uneasiness, or anger. When it took leave at last, the huge reptile merely rose from the bottom and swam off in a lumbering but powerful way, gliding upstream seemingly without effort under the steady propulsion of its undulating tail. Sarano, Deloire, and Noirot returned to their Zodiac, flushed with adrenaline, amazed by the extraordinary encounter, intoxicated by the realization that, to our knowledge, they were the first in history to film a saltwater crocodile underwater.

In Kakadu, about half the saltwater crocodile population leaves saltwater behind, ranging far up inland waterways, sharing river bottoms and billabongs with their freshwater cousins. When I visited Cornu and Blessington, and accompanied them to observe crocodile behavior, I felt as if my days in Kakadu were part of some time-warp return to the Age of Reptiles. Immense salties lay in the shade of bankside trees, making them difficult to see. Others patrolled the river or hung motionless in the water, exposing only their eyes.

The crocodile abundance we witnessed had been nearly wiped out by skin and meat hunters before crocodiles began receiving protected status in Australia in 1970. Conservationists worried that a creature whose lineage traced back 200 million years to the Mesozoic era was about to become locally extinct, perhaps disrupting an entire ecosystem in which the crocodile was a keystone predator. Today, the effort to protect these ancient reptiles is symbolic of the dramatic shift in public attitudes toward Australia's natural heritage.

One night, Cornu and Blessington accompanied park rangers in two small skiffs on a crocodile-counting mission down the East Alligator River. Wielding spotlights, the team scoured riverbanks for the telltale, ruby-red reflection of crocodile eyes. The monthly census trips have determined that there are about 400 crocodiles living along the East Alligator, a number authorities hope to expand.

Though hunting is no longer a threat, the crocodile population grows slowly because of natural checks. Only about twenty percent of saltwater crocodile eggs survive to hatch, and half of the hatchlings die within the first year under relentless predation by birds, fish, and larger crocodiles. To rebuild the population, wildlife management teams collect eggs from the wild and raise hatchlings under controlled conditions, then release the young back into the wild.

In parts of northern Australia, however, these efforts have spawned heated controversies. As crocodile populations have increased and reached maturity so, too, have reports of attacks on humans. In many cases, it is difficult to separate fact from fiction. Crocodiles have been reported jumping into boats, devouring fishermen, carrying away children. While many stories prove to be false, documented cases are also on the rise.

Jean-Michel examines Salvinia molesta, *an aquatic weed that has migrated from Brazil to Australia and Papua New Guinea, where it chokes streams through explosive growth and absorbs nutrients needed by indigenous plants and fish. At present, it has arrived in Kakadu Park, and has prompted treatment programs to eliminate it.*

Under the circumstances, wildlife managers struggle to maintain public support for their programs. Those who would reinstate wild creatures often find that their efforts produce conflicts between the short-term interests of humanity and the long-term health of an ecosystem. It is likely that Australians will face many difficult choices like this in coming decades as economic development comes face-to-face with projects to re-create the natural world.

The management schemes at Kakadu illustrate other dilemmas facing wildlife authorities across the continent. It is one thing to restore a native population to its former diversity, another to reorganize an environment invaded by alien species. At Kakadu, though the number of introduced species is generally quite low, a few immigrants have had patchy impacts on parklands, disturbing but not eliminating native flora and fauna. Yet, since the goal at Kakadu is to preserve the ancient environment, efforts are underway to remove several newcomers.

The aquatic fern *Salvinia molesta*, which has somehow made its way here from its native Brazil, has an immense capacity to reproduce by budding and can quickly choke waterways, while absorbing most of the water nutrients needed by other life. We saw the dramatic effects of salvinia along the Sepik River in Papua New Guinea, where it had not only overwhelmed river systems in some areas but had halted travel by natives in canoes. Experimental importation of a South American weevil, which feeds on salvinia, seemed to offer hope for the problem in Papua New Guinea and attempts to repeat the process have begun at Kakadu. Though salvinia has infested only a few waterways of the park, it remains a serious threat because of its potential to spread like a waterborne wildfire.

Another plant pest posing a danger to Kakadu is the giant prickly shrub *Mimosa pigra*, famed for its sensitivity. When touched, mimosa leaves close up. The distribution of mimosa from its origination in Central America may be in part the fascination with this curious trait. Directors of botanical gardens throughout the world have yearned to display the shrub, and in some places it has escaped the exhibits. Liberated, it often takes over a local plant community because of its rapid growth, its ability to withstand drought, and the fact that its seeds can float and thus disperse widely and quickly.

Though not yet a dire threat to Kakadu, the shrub has reached the edges of the park and caused enough consternation that four people are now employed full-time to patrol the park on mimosa search-and-destroy missions. Should thickets of mimosa get out of control, the first victims would likely be the magpie geese, whose remaining habitat would probably be overrun.

The presence of another exotic organism makes possible the potentially devastating invasion of the mimosa. In some parts of Kakadu, the opportunistic mimosa would face little competition from native plants, because they have been largely removed through the overgrazing of Asian water buffaloes. Imported from Indonesia early in the 19th century as beasts of burden, water buffaloes escaped captivity or were released, forming wild herds that still range about coastal floodplains of the Top End.

For some Australians, the buffaloes represent a resource. Their hides and meat have been harvested for a century. But the heavy creatures have a detrimental effect on fragile and wet floodplains, not only overgrazing in some areas, but also destroying native flora by compacting the soil, trampling delicate plants, rubbing trees forcefully enough to topple them, and consuming so much water in dry-season billabongs that native wildlife is often dangerously deprived. Their trails, wallows, and swimming channels have altered the ancient movement of water across parts of the floodplains.

While conservationists and harvesters argued over the future of the water buffaloes, the Australian government initiated a campaign to rid the country's cattle herds of two diseases—brucellosis and tuberculosis. As it happens, the virulency of these diseases among buffaloes is higher than among cattle, and the combination of disease eradication programs and conservation schemes has spelled a death warrant for the buffaloes.

To rid Kakadu of its estimated 20,000 water buffaloes, park managers have authorized mass killings by commercial contractors and, since this has largely proven impractical, the round-up and transport of herds to slaugh-

Using helicopters and jeeps, Kakadu Park Rangers drive water buffaloes into temporary holding pens. Early immigrants to Australia imported buffaloes as domestic animals, but over decades many herds escaped captivity to roam the wild, where their size and feeding habits have proven damaging to native habitats. Rangers now hope to round-up and ship an estimated 20,000 buffaloes from Kakadu.

terhouses. The mustering of water buffaloes is a spectacular operation. Like flying cowboys, helicopter pilots spot the herds and, in wildly acrobatic aerial maneuvers at treetop level, drive them toward corrals. On the ground, jeep-borne drovers race about through clouds of dust to channel the buffaloes through gates and into confinement. Eventually, authorities hope, the herculean effort to eradicate buffaloes will reduce their number to such an extent that extinction is inevitable.

The complexity of managing nature, however, has presented Kakadu's directors with a potential consequence of the buffalo removal that was not anticipated. Rangers told Cornu that with the decline of the buffalo herds, which long served as a meat supply for local crocodiles, the voracious predators would likely increase their attacks on tourists and fishermen.

Human presence in Kakadu evokes issues both troublesome and hopeful, and combines in a microcosm many of the knotty problems facing all of Australia. In the first place, Kakadu is an Aboriginal homeland, and many of its natural features are sacred to the Gagudju people, whose tenure here

covers perhaps 55,000 years. Aboriginal cave paintings in Kakadu may be 35,000 years old and, since they are regularly maintained by natives, probably represent the world's longest continuous record of this art form.

With the declaration of Kakadu as a national park, Australia ceded the land to the Gagudju, who in turn leased it back for use as a park. The effects upon traditional life have been considerable, perhaps foreshadowing the future of tribes elsewhere in Australia. Aboriginals have taken an active role in park management, serving not only as rangers but directing burnings in the manner of their ancestors.

The National Park and Wildlife Service pays the 350-member Gagudju tribe about $150,000 annually in lease fees. With money to spend, Gagudju are less dependent than other Aboriginals on welfare. Packaged goods from a supermarket in the park town of Jabiru increasingly replace such traditional fare as lizards and water-lily stems.

As park owners, the Gagudju have been drawn into decisions of national, even international importance. Before Kakadu was declared a national

Members of the Gagadju people dance near Jabiru, a town within Kakadu's boundaries. Like Uluru, Kakadu was deeded to the local Aboriginal people, who in turn leased it back to the government. The tribe receives about $150,000 annually in fees, as well as royalties and lease fees from mining conducted in the park.

park, uranium was discovered within its present boundaries. The riches proved to be of great consequence. Kakadu, it turns out, contains as much as ten percent of the world's known high-grade uranium.

Gagudju elders like Bill Neidje, who guided us about parts of the park, were consulted on the question of mining by officials of the government, including then Prime Minister Malcolm Fraser. Neidje told us that mine proponents promised the Gagudju enormous profits from mine royalties— about $2,000 per person annually. Enough, they told Neidje, to buy a car and a house.

A Gagadju man plays the traditional drone pipe instrument known as the didjeridu.

Permission was granted, and today near Mt. Brockman, believed by the Gagudju to be the dwelling place of the sacred Rainbow Snake, in the heart of Kakadu Park, an immense pit marks one of the largest uranium mines in the world. With Cornu and Blessington, I toured the Ranger Mine. Officials were open and forthright in answering our questions, and in permitting us access to mine facilities. We found the operation to be as careful in its processing and control of potentially deadly materials as any we had visited. Staff scientists constantly monitor park soils and waters, they take blood samples regularly from wildlife—and Gagudju living near the mine—in a genuine attempt to detect any release of toxic substances into the surrounding environment.

There are elaborate plans as well to restore the ancient ecosystem when the mine closes. Every structure will be removed, every road scraped away, and the land will be replanted with native vegetation. Some of this work has already begun, although mining will not be finished for another twenty-five years.

The Ranger Mine has made good also on its promises to the Gagudju. Some ninety million dollars in royalties (about four and a quarter percent of gross revenues) have enabled a tribal association to ensure the economic

Jean-Michel discusses the future of the Ranger Uranium Mine in Kakadu Park with mine manager Bob Cleary. Mine officials propose to fill the huge excavation with radioactive tailings and cap it over when the mine closes, assuring critics that the region will be safe for a thousand years. While finding the mine well run, the Cousteau team remained skeptical about the long-term future, since matter buried in the mine pit will remain dangerous for many thousands of years.

future of the tribe. The Gagudju now run two hotels of their own, as well as a school and medical clinic.

We were impressed by the dedication of the mine management to safety and by the honorable treatment they have extended to Aboriginals. At the same time, I left the mine harboring worries about the distant future. For one thing, the careful production methods of the mine mask an enormous contradiction. With a third of the world's reserves, Australia *sells* uranium for power generation only to Europe, Japan, and the United States, yet *bans* nuclear power at home. The profits stay, the perils are sent elsewhere. And while Ranger takes elaborate precautions with its ore, what prevents uranium from being converted for nuclear weaponry down the distribution line, after Ranger and the government of Australia no longer control the materials?

Also, mine manager Bob Cleary told me that the site will look untouched when Ranger evacuates the area, that radioactive mine tailings will be dumped into the pit and capped in such a way as to ensure the region's security for a thousand years at least. I believe the miners try assiduously to honor their trust, but they will leave behind matter still dangerous for many millennia. I left Kakadu pondering a supreme irony: here, where we are trying mightily to guard the purity of the past, we are providing the poison to contaminate the future.

As we departed Australia, a single story encapsulated for me the enduring antiquity and the biological vigor of the continent, and illustrated the priceless natural treasures Australians risk losing if they fail to protect vigilantly their unique natural world. It was set in Kakadu, a place rich in symbolism, a place where all of Australia's past and present seem embroiled in a chemical mix that will cast the shape of the future. And it was not my story, but Dick Murphy's.

During his early scouting mission through the park, Murphy had driven to the edge of the great escarpment fringing Kakadu and had parked along Nourlangie Creek. Monsoon rains had swollen the waterway and it overflowed its banks in several places. Murphy spent an entire day on foot, roaming with his camera, capturing as only a biologist can the emergence of new life as the Wet worked its annual magic across the floodplain. As dusk approached, Murphy realized that he was miles from his vehicle. By following the creek, he reasoned, he could still find the all-terrain truck in the dark. But as the moonless night fell, spreading a blackness unbroken by light in any direction, Murphy found it difficult to determine what was creek and what was floodplain. His only option was to remove his shoes and feel his way along the sandy creek bed.

Murphy's mind wandered. He had seen cave paintings along the edge of the escarpment during the day. Now, he thought about the fact that thousands of generations of Aboriginals had trod this same ground, fished this creek, celebrated the return of 50,000 wet seasons like this one. He brushed against a tree, knocking loose an ant nest. Quickly brushing the swarming colony from his chest, he was reminded of the incredible richness and array of Kakadu's tropical life. It struck him that he was as alone and lost in time as any Aboriginal who might have felt his way along this same creek in an era so far removed from the present that neither farming nor the wheel had yet been invented. In the darkness thousands of miles away, scholars and politicians fretted over a deteriorating world economy. Eastern Europeans reveled in the fall of a system called communism. But these things bore little meaning for a lonely soul engulfed in the Kakadu night.

And as he walked, frogs enlivened by the wet season began to croak. The sounds of a few frogs seemed to cue others, and the chorus multiplied. And multiplied. Soon it seemed as if every sound within the capacity of the frog anatomy was wafting about Murphy—chirps, wheezes, moans, clacks, squeals, rumbles, clicks, pops—a vast symphony arising from millions of frog throats. The world economy was in shambles and Europe was in upheaval, and none of that seemed more or less important than the amassed voices of frogs instinctively celebrating the regeneration of their world. The political machinations of human civilization would cause cyclical changes as long as humanity endured, approximating a pulsed equilibium similiar to that of Kakadu's ancient seasonal rituals of life and death and life and death. The countless words reverberating through the media of the human world, so fraught with profundity, were no more eloquent in their evocation of cosmic meaning than the murmur of frogs in the darkness.

In the enveloping symphony of the frogs was the resonance of the ages, the song of hope and anticipation embodied in every creature, the voice of earth's life force itself. Murphy reached his car and quietly drove back to the present through the musical darkness of Kakadu.

We would like to thank five expedition members in particular: chief diver Stephen Arrington, whose journals enabled us to reconstruct *Alcyone*'s adventures in Australian waters; Captain Nicholas Dourassoff, whose logs and telexes from *Alcyone* supplied vital information; biologist François Sarano, who researched the Great Barrier Reef and reviewed our chapter describing the resulting mission; and cinematographers-photographers Didier Noirot and Chuck Davis, who recalled for us details of many Cousteau team experiences on the Great Barrier Reef and in Western Australia.

Thanks also to Dr. Richard C. Murphy, for his invaluable suggestions and for his accounts of personal observations in Australia; to Neal Shapiro and Elliott Cowand, whose research helped shape the entire expedition; and to Karen Brazeau and Ian Chapman, whose logistical work in the field enabled dozens of expedition members to gather data and film throughout the great southern continent.

We are deeply indebted to Judy Brody, whose sharp eye and tireless efforts contributed to the photographic quality of the book, and to Lesley High, whose behind-the-scenes work made the book a reality.

We are grateful as well to Cousteau writers Paula DiPerna and Mary Batten, from whose expedition articles and scripts we drew important material.

Kind thanks also to the Australian Tourism Commission, the Australian Institute of Marine Science and Dr. Michel Pichon, the Great Barrier Reef Marine Park Authority, the Queensland Department of Environment, Conservation and Tourism, the Western Australian Tourism Commission, the Forestry Commission of Tasmania, and the Pitjantjatjara and Bardi councils.

JEAN-MICHEL COUSTEAU AND MOSE RICHARDS

INDEX

Pages in *italics* refer to illustrations and captions

PHOTO CREDITS

Stephen Arrington: 53, 62, 74, 92, 93, 95, 103, 132, 144–145, 147, 149, 151, 153
Catherine S. Cornu: 165, 170
Anne-Marie Cousteau: 6–7, 88, 90, 91, 94, 96–97, 98, 99, 100–101, 105 (top), 107, 108, 110, 112, 114, 115, 116, 117, 120, 121, 124–125, 127, 129, 130, 134–135, 137, 138, 139, 141
Chuck Davis: 2–3, 4–5, 47, 48–49, 56, 57, 59, 61, 63, 64, 65, 67, 70, 72, 77, 79, 82, 83, 85, 87, 113 (top), 152
Richard C. Murphy: 1, 36, 44, 51, 54–55, 58, 68, 71, 76, 104, 105 (bottom), 154, 156 (bottom), 157, 159, 162
Didier Noirot: 8, 12–13, 15, 16, 17, 18, 19, 22, 23 (bottom), 24, 25, 27, 28, 29, 30, 32–33, 34, 35, 37, 39, 40–41, 106, 160 (bottom), 161
Sylvain Pascaud: 113 (bottom)
François Quillard: 156 (top), 160 (top), 167, 168, 169
Veronique Sarano: 23 (top)
Bob Talbot: 86
Capkin Van Alphen: 78

Map on page 11 created by Christine Edwards